Service Line
Complete Self-Assessment Guide

C000060633

The guidance in this Self-Assessment is based on Service Line best practices and standards in business process architecture, design and quality management. The guidance is also based on the professional judgment of the individual collaborators listed in the Acknowledgments.

Notice of rights

Trademarks

Many of the designations used by manufacturers and sellers to distinguish their products are claimed as trademarks. Where those designations appear in this book, and the publisher was aware of a trademark claim, the designations appear as requested by the owner of the trademark. All other product names and services identified throughout this book are used in editorial fashion only and for the benefit of such companies with no intention of infringement of the trademark. No such use, or the use of any trade name, is intended to convey endorsement or other affiliation with this book.

Table of Contents

About The Art of Service

The Art of Service, Business Process Architects since 2000, is dedicated to helping stakeholders achieve excellence.

Defining, designing, creating, and implementing a process to solve a stakeholders challenge or meet an objective is the most valuable role... In EVERY group, company, organization and department.

Unless you're talking a one-time, single-use project, there should be a process. Whether that process is managed and implemented by humans, AI, or a combination of the two, it needs to be designed by someone with a complex enough perspective to ask the right questions.

Someone capable of asking the right questions and step back and say, 'What are we really trying to accomplish here? And is there a different way to look at it?'

With The Art of Service's Standard Requirements Self-Assessments, we empower people who can do just that — whether their title is marketer, entrepreneur, manager, salesperson, consultant, Business Process Manager, executive assistant, IT Manager, CIO etc... —they are the people who rule the future. They are people who watch the process as it happens, and ask the right questions to make the process work better.

Contact us when you need any support with this Self-Assessment and any help with templates, blue-prints and examples of standard documents you might need:

http://theartofservice.com
service@theartofservice.com

Acknowledgments

This checklist was developed under the auspices of The Art of Service, chaired by Gerardus Blokdyk.

Representatives from several client companies participated in the preparation of this Self-Assessment.

In addition, we are thankful for the design and printing services provided.

Included Resources - how to access

Included with your purchase of the book is the Service Line Self-Assessment Spreadsheet Dashboard which contains all questions and Self-Assessment areas and auto-generates insights, graphs, and project RACI planning - all with examples to get you started right away.

How? Simply send an email to
access@theartofservice.com
with this books' title in the subject to get the Service Line Self Assessment Tool right away.

You will receive the following contents with New and Updated specific criteria:

- The latest quick edition of the book in PDF

- The latest complete edition of the book in PDF, which criteria correspond to the criteria in...

- The Self-Assessment Excel Dashboard, and...

- Example pre-filled Self-Assessment Excel Dashboard to get familiar with results generation

- In-depth specific Checklists covering the topic

- Project management checklists and templates to assist with implementation

INCLUDES LIFETIME SELF ASSESSMENT UPDATES

Every self assessment comes with Lifetime Updates and Lifetime Free Updated Books. Lifetime Updates is an industry-first feature which allows you to receive verified self assessment updates, ensuring you always have the most accurate information at your fingertips.

Get it now- you will be glad you did - do it now, before you forget.

Send an email to **access@theartofservice.com** with this books' title in the subject to get the Service Line Self Assessment Tool right away.

Your feedback is invaluable to us

If you recently bought this book, we would love to hear from you! You can do this by writing a review on amazon (or the online store where you purchased this book) about your last purchase! As part of our continual service improvement process, we love to hear real client experiences and feedback.

How does it work?
To post a review on Amazon, just log in to your account and click on the Create Your Own Review button (under Customer Reviews) of the relevant product page. You can find examples of product reviews in Amazon. If you purchased from another online store, simply follow their procedures.

What happens when I submit my review?
Once you have submitted your review, send us an email at review@theartofservice.com with the link to your review so we can properly thank you for your feedback.

Purpose of this Self-Assessment

This Self-Assessment has been developed to improve understanding of the requirements and elements of Service Line, based on best practices and standards in business process architecture, design and quality management.

It is designed to allow for a rapid Self-Assessment to determine how closely existing management practices and procedures correspond to the elements of the Self-Assessment.

The criteria of requirements and elements of Service Line have been rephrased in the format of a Self-Assessment questionnaire, with a seven-criterion scoring system, as explained in this document.

In this format, even with limited background knowledge of

Service Line, a manager can quickly review existing operations to determine how they measure up to the standards. This in turn can serve as the starting point of a 'gap analysis' to identify management tools or system elements that might usefully be implemented in the organization to help improve overall performance.

How to use the Self-Assessment

On the following pages are a series of questions to identify to what extent your Service Line initiative is complete in comparison to the requirements set in standards.

To facilitate answering the questions, there is a space in front of each question to enter a score on a scale of '1' to '5'.

1 Strongly Disagree

2 Disagree

3 Neutral

4 Agree

5 Strongly Agree

Read the question and rate it with the following in front of mind:

**'In my belief,
the answer to this question is clearly defined'.**

There are two ways in which you can choose to interpret this statement;
1. how aware are you that the answer to the question is clearly defined
2. for more in-depth analysis you can choose to gather

evidence and confirm the answer to the question. This obviously will take more time, most Self-Assessment users opt for the first way to interpret the question and dig deeper later on based on the outcome of the overall Self-Assessment.

A score of '1' would mean that the answer is not clear at all, where a '5' would mean the answer is crystal clear and defined. Leave emtpy when the question is not applicable or you don't want to answer it, you can skip it without affecting your score. Write your score in the space provided.

After you have responded to all the appropriate statements in each section, compute your average score for that section, using the formula provided, and round to the nearest tenth. Then transfer to the corresponding spoke in the Service Line Scorecard on the second next page of the Self-Assessment.

Your completed Service Line Scorecard will give you a clear presentation of which Service Line areas need attention.

Service Line
Scorecard Example

Example of how the finalized Scorecard can look like:

Service Line Scorecard

Your Scores:

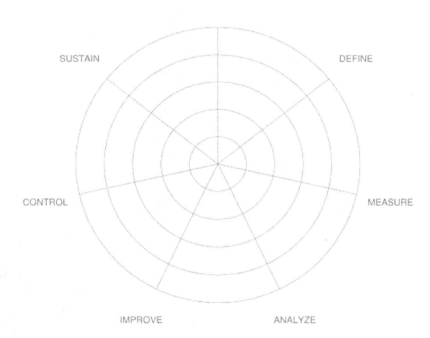

BEGINNING OF THE SELF-ASSESSMENT:

CRITERION #1: RECOGNIZE

INTENT: Be aware of the need for change. Recognize that there is an unfavorable variation, problem or symptom.

In my belief, the answer to this question is clearly defined:

5 Strongly Agree

4 Agree

3 Neutral

2 Disagree

1 Strongly Disagree

1. What information do users need?
<--- Score

2. Who should resolve the Service Line issues?
<--- Score

3. As a sponsor, customer or management, how important is it to meet goals, objectives?
<--- Score

4. Do you know what you need to know about Service Line?
<--- Score

5. What activities does the governance board need to consider?
<--- Score

6. What needs to be done?
<--- Score

7. What is the extent or complexity of the Service Line problem?
<--- Score

8. Will Service Line deliverables need to be tested and, if so, by whom?
<--- Score

9. Think about the people you identified for your Service Line project and the project responsibilities you would assign to them, what kind of training do you think they would need to perform these responsibilities effectively?
<--- Score

10. What do you need to start doing?
<--- Score

11. Which needs are not included or involved?
<--- Score

12. Who are your key stakeholders who need to sign off?
<--- Score

13. Are employees recognized or rewarded for performance that demonstrates the highest levels of integrity?
<--- Score

14. What tools and technologies are needed for a custom Service Line project?
<--- Score

15. What does Service Line success mean to the stakeholders?
<--- Score

16. Are losses recognized in a timely manner?
<--- Score

17. Will a response program recognize when a crisis occurs and provide some level of response?
<--- Score

18. How do you assess your Service Line workforce capability and capacity needs, including skills, competencies, and staffing levels?
<--- Score

19. Do you need to avoid or amend any Service Line activities?
<--- Score

20. What is the problem and/or vulnerability?
<--- Score

21. Are there recognized Service Line problems?
<--- Score

22. Why is this needed?
<--- Score

23. What should be considered when identifying available resources, constraints, and deadlines?
<--- Score

24. How do you recognize an objection?
<--- Score

25. What training and capacity building actions are needed to implement proposed reforms?
<--- Score

26. Do you recognize Service Line achievements?
<--- Score

27. Who defines the rules in relation to any given issue?
<--- Score

28. To what extent does each concerned units management team recognize Service Line as an effective investment?
<--- Score

29. What is the smallest subset of the problem you can usefully solve?
<--- Score

30. How many trainings, in total, are needed?
<--- Score

31. Why the need?
<--- Score

32. Does your organization need more Service Line education?
<--- Score

33. What do employees need in the short term?
<--- Score

34. Looking at each person individually – does every one have the qualities which are needed to work in this group?
<--- Score

35. What extra resources will you need?
<--- Score

36. Will it solve real problems?
<--- Score

37. Which information does the Service Line business case need to include?
<--- Score

38. Which issues are too important to ignore?
<--- Score

39. How are training requirements identified?
<--- Score

40. What situation(s) led to this Service Line Self Assessment?
<--- Score

41. How do you identify the kinds of information that you will need?
<--- Score

42. What are the clients issues and concerns?
<--- Score

43. Are controls defined to recognize and contain problems?
<--- Score

44. What else needs to be measured?
<--- Score

45. Are you dealing with any of the same issues today as yesterday? What can you do about this?
<--- Score

46. To what extent would your organization benefit from being recognized as a award recipient?
<--- Score

47. How do you recognize an Service Line objection?
<--- Score

48. Are there regulatory / compliance issues?
<--- Score

49. What resources or support might you need?
<--- Score

50. Do you have/need 24-hour access to key personnel?
<--- Score

51. Are problem definition and motivation clearly presented?
<--- Score

52. What Service Line events should you attend?

<--- Score

53. Where is training needed?
<--- Score

54. Who needs to know?
<--- Score

55. Is it clear when you think of the day ahead of you what activities and tasks you need to complete?
<--- Score

56. Where do you need to exercise leadership?
<--- Score

57. Can management personnel recognize the monetary benefit of Service Line?
<--- Score

58. Are there any revenue recognition issues?
<--- Score

59. Do you need different information or graphics?
<--- Score

60. How are you going to measure success?
<--- Score

61. Are your goals realistic? Do you need to redefine your problem? Perhaps the problem has changed or maybe you have reached your goal and need to set a new one?
<--- Score

62. Consider your own Service Line project, what types of organizational problems do you think might

be causing or affecting your problem, based on the work done so far?
<--- Score

63. What Service Line problem should be solved?
<--- Score

64. What vendors make products that address the Service Line needs?
<--- Score

65. How much are sponsors, customers, partners, stakeholders involved in Service Line? In other words, what are the risks, if Service Line does not deliver successfully?
<--- Score

66. Who needs what information?
<--- Score

67. What creative shifts do you need to take?
<--- Score

68. Did you miss any major Service Line issues?
<--- Score

69. What Service Line coordination do you need?
<--- Score

70. What are the timeframes required to resolve each of the issues/problems?
<--- Score

71. What are the minority interests and what amount of minority interests can be recognized?
<--- Score

72. Are there any specific expectations or concerns about the Service Line team, Service Line itself?
<--- Score

73. How can auditing be a preventative security measure?
<--- Score

74. What problems are you facing and how do you consider Service Line will circumvent those obstacles?
<--- Score

75. How do you take a forward-looking perspective in identifying Service Line research related to market response and models?
<--- Score

76. Would you recognize a threat from the inside?
<--- Score

77. Does Service Line create potential expectations in other areas that need to be recognized and considered?
<--- Score

78. Who needs to know about Service Line?
<--- Score

79. Who else hopes to benefit from it?
<--- Score

80. Who needs budgets?
<--- Score

81. Are employees recognized for desired behaviors?

<--- Score

82. Is it needed?
<--- Score

83. Have you identified your Service Line key performance indicators?
<--- Score

84. What are the expected benefits of Service Line to the stakeholder?
<--- Score

85. What Service Line capabilities do you need?
<--- Score

86. How are the Service Line's objectives aligned to the group's overall stakeholder strategy?
<--- Score

87. When a Service Line manager recognizes a problem, what options are available?
<--- Score

88. What prevents you from making the changes you know will make you a more effective Service Line leader?
<--- Score

89. What needs to stay?
<--- Score

90. What is the problem or issue?
<--- Score

91. Does the problem have ethical dimensions?

<--- Score

92. What are the stakeholder objectives to be achieved with Service Line?
<--- Score

93. What would happen if Service Line weren't done?
<--- Score

Add up total points for this section:
_ _ _ _ _ = Total points for this section

Divided by: _ _ _ _ _ _ (number of statements answered) = _ _ _ _ _ _
Average score for this section

Transfer your score to the Service Line Index at the beginning of the Self-Assessment.

CRITERION #2: DEFINE:

INTENT: Formulate the stakeholder problem. Define the problem, needs and objectives.

In my belief, the answer to this question is clearly defined:

5 Strongly Agree

4 Agree

3 Neutral

2 Disagree

1 Strongly Disagree

1. What customer feedback methods were used to solicit their input?
<--- Score

2. Who defines (or who defined) the rules and roles?
<--- Score

3. What are the core elements of the Service Line business case?

<--- Score

4. What are the dynamics of the communication plan?
<--- Score

5. How do you keep key subject matter experts in the loop?
<--- Score

6. How and when will the baselines be defined?
<--- Score

7. Have specific policy objectives been defined?
<--- Score

8. Are team charters developed?
<--- Score

9. Is special Service Line user knowledge required?
<--- Score

10. Has a high-level 'as is' process map been completed, verified and validated?
<--- Score

11. How do you manage unclear Service Line requirements?
<--- Score

12. How do you hand over Service Line context?
<--- Score

13. Are there any constraints known that bear on the ability to perform Service Line work? How is the team addressing them?
<--- Score

14. Have all basic functions of Service Line been defined?
<--- Score

15. What is out-of-scope initially?
<--- Score

16. Who are the Service Line improvement team members, including Management Leads and Coaches?
<--- Score

17. If substitutes have been appointed, have they been briefed on the Service Line goals and received regular communications as to the progress to date?
<--- Score

18. Who is gathering information?
<--- Score

19. What constraints exist that might impact the team?
<--- Score

20. Who approved the Service Line scope?
<--- Score

21. Is the Service Line scope complete and appropriately sized?
<--- Score

22. When is the estimated completion date?
<--- Score

23. How do you build the right business case?

<--- Score

24. Is the Service Line scope manageable?
<--- Score

25. Are roles and responsibilities formally defined?
<--- Score

26. Is Service Line required?
<--- Score

27. Will team members perform Service Line work when assigned and in a timely fashion?
<--- Score

28. What are the tasks and definitions?
<--- Score

29. What are (control) requirements for Service Line Information?
<--- Score

30. Has the improvement team collected the 'voice of the customer' (obtained feedback – qualitative and quantitative)?
<--- Score

31. Do you all define Service Line in the same way?
<--- Score

32. What is the scope?
<--- Score

33. Is the improvement team aware of the different versions of a process: what they think it is vs. what it actually is vs. what it should be vs. what it could be?

<--- Score

34. How do you manage changes in Service Line requirements?
<--- Score

35. Do you have organizational privacy requirements?
<--- Score

36. Is there a critical path to deliver Service Line results?
<--- Score

37. What is the definition of success?
<--- Score

38. How do you gather Service Line requirements?
<--- Score

39. Is it clearly defined in and to your organization what you do?
<--- Score

40. How often are the team meetings?
<--- Score

41. Are all requirements met?
<--- Score

42. How will variation in the actual durations of each activity be dealt with to ensure that the expected Service Line results are met?
<--- Score

43. What is the worst case scenario?
<--- Score

44. When is/was the Service Line start date?
<--- Score

45. In what way can you redefine the criteria of choice clients have in your category in your favor?
<--- Score

46. What is out of scope?
<--- Score

47. How would you define the culture at your organization, how susceptible is it to Service Line changes?
<--- Score

48. What intelligence can you gather?
<--- Score

49. Is the team formed and are team leaders (Coaches and Management Leads) assigned?
<--- Score

50. What is the context?
<--- Score

51. How would you define Service Line leadership?
<--- Score

52. Are different versions of process maps needed to account for the different types of inputs?
<--- Score

53. What are the Service Line use cases?
<--- Score

54. Is the team sponsored by a champion or stakeholder leader?

<--- Score

55. Is full participation by members in regularly held team meetings guaranteed?

<--- Score

56. What defines best in class?

<--- Score

57. Does the team have regular meetings?

<--- Score

58. Is there regularly 100% attendance at the team meetings? If not, have appointed substitutes attended to preserve cross-functionality and full representation?

<--- Score

59. What Service Line services do you require?

<--- Score

60. Is data collected and displayed to better understand customer(s) critical needs and requirements.

<--- Score

61. What was the context?

<--- Score

62. How will the Service Line team and the group measure complete success of Service Line?

<--- Score

63. Has everyone on the team, including the team

leaders, been properly trained?
<--- Score

64. What are the rough order estimates on cost savings/opportunities that Service Line brings?
<--- Score

65. How did the Service Line manager receive input to the development of a Service Line improvement plan and the estimated completion dates/times of each activity?
<--- Score

66. Is the team equipped with available and reliable resources?
<--- Score

67. Has your scope been defined?
<--- Score

68. How do you manage scope?
<--- Score

69. What are the compelling stakeholder reasons for embarking on Service Line?
<--- Score

70. Why are you doing Service Line and what is the scope?
<--- Score

71. What information do you gather?
<--- Score

72. Has anyone else (internal or external to the group) attempted to solve this problem or a similar one

before? If so, what knowledge can be leveraged from these previous efforts?
<--- Score

73. Is Service Line currently on schedule according to the plan?
<--- Score

74. Are the Service Line requirements testable?
<--- Score

75. What would be the goal or target for a Service Line's improvement team?
<--- Score

76. How are consistent Service Line definitions important?
<--- Score

77. What are the requirements for audit information?
<--- Score

78. When are meeting minutes sent out? Who is on the distribution list?
<--- Score

79. How have you defined all Service Line requirements first?
<--- Score

80. What critical content must be communicated – who, what, when, where, and how?
<--- Score

81. Is there a Service Line management charter, including stakeholder case, problem and

goal statements, scope, milestones, roles and
responsibilities, communication plan?
<--- Score

82. Is there a completed SIPOC representation,
describing the Suppliers, Inputs, Process, Outputs, and
Customers?
<--- Score

83. Do you have a Service Line success story or case
study ready to tell and share?
<--- Score

84. What gets examined?
<--- Score

85. How was the 'as is' process map developed,
reviewed, verified and validated?
<--- Score

86. Is there a completed, verified, and validated high-
level 'as is' (not 'should be' or 'could be') stakeholder
process map?
<--- Score

87. How do you gather requirements?
<--- Score

88. What key stakeholder process output measure(s)
does Service Line leverage and how?
<--- Score

89. What is the scope of the Service Line work?
<--- Score

90. How can the value of Service Line be defined?

<--- Score

91. Are task requirements clearly defined?
<--- Score

92. How is the team tracking and documenting its work?
<--- Score

93. Are required metrics defined, what are they?
<--- Score

94. What are the Roles and Responsibilities for each team member and its leadership? Where is this documented?
<--- Score

95. Is the current 'as is' process being followed? If not, what are the discrepancies?
<--- Score

96. What is in the scope and what is not in scope?
<--- Score

97. Where can you gather more information?
<--- Score

98. Are audit criteria, scope, frequency and methods defined?
<--- Score

99. Are there different segments of customers?
<--- Score

100. Are improvement team members fully trained on Service Line?

<--- Score

101. What are the boundaries of the scope? What is in bounds and what is not? What is the start point? What is the stop point?
<--- Score

102. How do you gather the stories?
<--- Score

103. What information should you gather?
<--- Score

104. What sort of initial information to gather?
<--- Score

105. What happens if Service Line's scope changes?
<--- Score

106. Will team members regularly document their Service Line work?
<--- Score

107. What baselines are required to be defined and managed?
<--- Score

108. What is a worst-case scenario for losses?
<--- Score

109. What Service Line requirements should be gathered?
<--- Score

110. What is the scope of Service Line?
<--- Score

111. Are customer(s) identified and segmented according to their different needs and requirements?
<--- Score

112. Are accountability and ownership for Service Line clearly defined?
<--- Score

113. Is there any additional Service Line definition of success?
<--- Score

114. The political context: who holds power?
<--- Score

115. Has the Service Line work been fairly and/ or equitably divided and delegated among team members who are qualified and capable to perform the work? Has everyone contributed?
<--- Score

116. Is the team adequately staffed with the desired cross-functionality? If not, what additional resources are available to the team?
<--- Score

117. Is Service Line linked to key stakeholder goals and objectives?
<--- Score

118. Has the direction changed at all during the course of Service Line? If so, when did it change and why?
<--- Score

119. Have all of the relationships been defined properly?
<--- Score

120. What scope do you want your strategy to cover?
<--- Score

121. How does the Service Line manager ensure against scope creep?
<--- Score

122. Who is gathering Service Line information?
<--- Score

123. Are resources adequate for the scope?
<--- Score

124. Are approval levels defined for contracts and supplements to contracts?
<--- Score

125. Are stakeholder processes mapped?
<--- Score

126. Is there a clear Service Line case definition?
<--- Score

127. Have the customer needs been translated into specific, measurable requirements? How?
<--- Score

128. How do you think the partners involved in Service Line would have defined success?
<--- Score

129. Has a project plan, Gantt chart, or similar been

developed/completed?
<--- Score

130. What scope to assess?
<--- Score

131. What sources do you use to gather information for a Service Line study?
<--- Score

132. What specifically is the problem? Where does it occur? When does it occur? What is its extent?
<--- Score

133. Has/have the customer(s) been identified?
<--- Score

134. Do the problem and goal statements meet the SMART criteria (specific, measurable, attainable, relevant, and time-bound)?
<--- Score

135. Is the work to date meeting requirements?
<--- Score

136. How do you catch Service Line definition inconsistencies?
<--- Score

137. Scope of sensitive information?
<--- Score

138. Has a team charter been developed and communicated?
<--- Score

139. What knowledge or experience is required?
<--- Score

Add up total points for this section:
_ _ _ _ _ = Total points for this section

Divided by: _ _ _ _ _ _ (number of
statements answered) = _ _ _ _ _ _
Average score for this section

Transfer your score to the Service Line
Index at the beginning of the Self-
Assessment.

CRITERION #3: MEASURE:

INTENT: Gather the correct data.
Measure the current performance and
evolution of the situation.

In my belief, the answer to this
question is clearly defined:

5 Strongly Agree

4 Agree

3 Neutral

2 Disagree

1 Strongly Disagree

1. What are the costs of delaying Service Line action?
<--- Score

2. Is it possible to estimate the impact of
unanticipated complexity such as wrong or failed
assumptions, feedback, etcetera on proposed
reforms?
<--- Score

3. How will success or failure be measured?
<--- Score

4. What does verifying compliance entail?
<--- Score

5. What is an unallowable cost?
<--- Score

6. How can a Service Line test verify your ideas or assumptions?
<--- Score

7. Who pays the cost?
<--- Score

8. How do you verify performance?
<--- Score

9. When a disaster occurs, who gets priority?
<--- Score

10. What are your key Service Line organizational performance measures, including key short and longer-term financial measures?
<--- Score

11. How do you verify Service Line completeness and accuracy?
<--- Score

12. Does the Service Line task fit the client's priorities?
<--- Score

13. How do you verify your resources?
<--- Score

14. What are the costs?
<--- Score

15. What are your primary costs, revenues, assets?
<--- Score

16. Which measures and indicators matter?
<--- Score

17. What is the cost of rework?
<--- Score

18. How do you aggregate measures across priorities?
<--- Score

19. What potential environmental factors impact the Service Line effort?
<--- Score

20. Do you aggressively reward and promote the people who have the biggest impact on creating excellent Service Line services/products?
<--- Score

21. What drives O&M cost?
<--- Score

22. Have you included everything in your Service Line cost models?
<--- Score

23. How is progress measured?
<--- Score

24. Which Service Line impacts are significant?

<--- Score

25. What is the total cost related to deploying Service Line, including any consulting or professional services?
<--- Score

26. How are costs allocated?
<--- Score

27. Do you have an issue in getting priority?
<--- Score

28. How will costs be allocated?
<--- Score

29. Are there measurements based on task performance?
<--- Score

30. What is your Service Line quality cost segregation study?
<--- Score

31. Where can you go to verify the info?
<--- Score

32. Have design-to-cost goals been established?
<--- Score

33. Among the Service Line product and service cost to be estimated, which is considered hardest to estimate?
<--- Score

34. Are missed Service Line opportunities costing your

organization money?
<--- Score

35. What is the Service Line business impact?
<--- Score

36. Why do you expend time and effort to implement measurement, for whom?
<--- Score

37. What evidence is there and what is measured?
<--- Score

38. What are the strategic priorities for this year?
<--- Score

39. What causes investor action?
<--- Score

40. What methods are feasible and acceptable to estimate the impact of reforms?
<--- Score

41. Where is it measured?
<--- Score

42. What disadvantage does this cause for the user?
<--- Score

43. Why do the measurements/indicators matter?
<--- Score

44. What is the cause of any Service Line gaps?
<--- Score

45. Are the units of measure consistent?

<--- Score

46. How can you reduce the costs of obtaining inputs?
<--- Score

47. Are there competing Service Line priorities?
<--- Score

48. How do you measure lifecycle phases?
<--- Score

49. How do you verify and develop ideas and innovations?
<--- Score

50. How do you prevent mis-estimating cost?
<--- Score

51. What details are required of the Service Line cost structure?
<--- Score

52. Are the Service Line benefits worth its costs?
<--- Score

53. How frequently do you track Service Line measures?
<--- Score

54. What are you verifying?
<--- Score

55. How do you verify the authenticity of the data and information used?
<--- Score

56. Are actual costs in line with budgeted costs?
<--- Score

57. What is measured? Why?
<--- Score

58. What are the Service Line investment costs?
<--- Score

59. When are costs are incurred?
<--- Score

60. What relevant entities could be measured?
<--- Score

61. What can be used to verify compliance?
<--- Score

62. Who is involved in verifying compliance?
<--- Score

63. Are supply costs steady or fluctuating?
<--- Score

64. How do you measure efficient delivery of Service
Line services?
<--- Score

65. What do people want to verify?
<--- Score

66. Do you verify that corrective actions were taken?
<--- Score

67. How can you reduce costs?
<--- Score

68. How can you measure Service Line in a systematic way?
<--- Score

69. Are there any easy-to-implement alternatives to Service Line? Sometimes other solutions are available that do not require the cost implications of a full-blown project?
<--- Score

70. Does management have the right priorities among projects?
<--- Score

71. How can you manage cost down?
<--- Score

72. How will you measure your Service Line effectiveness?
<--- Score

73. What are the costs of reform?
<--- Score

74. What harm might be caused?
<--- Score

75. Are you taking your company in the direction of better and revenue or cheaper and cost?
<--- Score

76. How much does it cost?
<--- Score

77. How frequently do you verify your Service Line

strategy?
<--- Score

78. Has a cost center been established?
<--- Score

79. Which costs should be taken into account?
<--- Score

80. Do the benefits outweigh the costs?
<--- Score

81. Will Service Line have an impact on current business continuity, disaster recovery processes and/or infrastructure?
<--- Score

82. Do you have a flow diagram of what happens?
<--- Score

83. What happens if cost savings do not materialize?
<--- Score

84. What would be a real cause for concern?
<--- Score

85. How do you verify if Service Line is built right?
<--- Score

86. What users will be impacted?
<--- Score

87. How will effects be measured?
<--- Score

88. What would it cost to replace your technology?

<--- Score

89. When should you bother with diagrams?
<--- Score

90. How sensitive must the Service Line strategy be to cost?
<--- Score

91. What is your decision requirements diagram?
<--- Score

92. Have you made assumptions about the shape of the future, particularly its impact on your customers and competitors?
<--- Score

93. What are allowable costs?
<--- Score

94. How do you verify and validate the Service Line data?
<--- Score

95. How to cause the change?
<--- Score

96. How do you measure variability?
<--- Score

97. At what cost?
<--- Score

98. What are the uncertainties surrounding estimates of impact?
<--- Score

99. How do you quantify and qualify impacts?
<--- Score

100. How do your measurements capture actionable Service Line information for use in exceeding your customers expectations and securing your customers engagement?
<--- Score

101. Was a business case (cost/benefit) developed?
<--- Score

102. What tests verify requirements?
<--- Score

103. What could cause you to change course?
<--- Score

104. How long to keep data and how to manage retention costs?
<--- Score

105. Are Service Line vulnerabilities categorized and prioritized?
<--- Score

106. Do you effectively measure and reward individual and team performance?
<--- Score

107. What could cause delays in the schedule?
<--- Score

108. Is there an opportunity to verify requirements?
<--- Score

109. Is the cost worth the Service Line effort ?
<--- Score

110. How do you verify the Service Line requirements quality?
<--- Score

111. What are the types and number of measures to use?
<--- Score

112. Are you aware of what could cause a problem?
<--- Score

113. How is performance measured?
<--- Score

114. Do you have any cost Service Line limitation requirements?
<--- Score

115. What measurements are being captured?
<--- Score

116. How is the value delivered by Service Line being measured?
<--- Score

117. What measurements are possible, practicable and meaningful?
<--- Score

118. What causes extra work or rework?
<--- Score

119. Who should receive measurement reports?
<--- Score

120. What does your operating model cost?
<--- Score

121. How do you measure success?
<--- Score

122. How will your organization measure success?
<--- Score

123. What are hidden Service Line quality costs?
<--- Score

124. What are the costs and benefits?
<--- Score

125. What are the estimated costs of proposed changes?
<--- Score

126. How are measurements made?
<--- Score

127. Does a Service Line quantification method exist?
<--- Score

128. What do you measure and why?
<--- Score

129. What is the total fixed cost?
<--- Score

130. How will measures be used to manage and adapt?

<--- Score

131. Are you able to realize any cost savings?
<--- Score

132. What does losing customers cost your organization?
<--- Score

133. Where is the cost?
<--- Score

134. How can you measure the performance?
<--- Score

135. What does a Test Case verify?
<--- Score

136. What are your operating costs?
<--- Score

137. What are the current costs of the Service Line process?
<--- Score

138. Are the measurements objective?
<--- Score

139. What are the operational costs after Service Line deployment?
<--- Score

Add up total points for this section:
_____ = Total points for this section

Divided by: _____ (number of

statements answered) = _ _ _ _ _ _
Average score for this section

Transfer your score to the Service Line
Index at the beginning of the Self-
Assessment.

CRITERION #4: ANALYZE:

INTENT: Analyze causes, assumptions and hypotheses.

In my belief, the answer to this question is clearly defined:

5 Strongly Agree

4 Agree

3 Neutral

2 Disagree

1 Strongly Disagree

1. Is the Service Line process severely broken such that a re-design is necessary?
<--- Score

2. What Service Line data will be collected?
<--- Score

3. How do mission and objectives affect the Service Line processes of your organization?
<--- Score

4. What do you need to qualify?
<--- Score

5. What tools were used to generate the list of possible causes?
<--- Score

6. Who will facilitate the team and process?
<--- Score

7. How can risk management be tied procedurally to process elements?
<--- Score

8. What are your outputs?
<--- Score

9. How does the organization define, manage, and improve its Service Line processes?
<--- Score

10. Are you missing Service Line opportunities?
<--- Score

11. What output to create?
<--- Score

12. What kind of crime could a potential new hire have committed that would not only not disqualify him/her from being hired by your organization, but would actually indicate that he/she might be a particularly good fit?
<--- Score

13. What is the Value Stream Mapping?

<--- Score

14. Is there any way to speed up the process?
<--- Score

15. What resources go in to get the desired output?
<--- Score

16. Should you invest in industry-recognized qualifications?
<--- Score

17. Is there an established change management process?
<--- Score

18. Do several people in different organizational units assist with the Service Line process?
<--- Score

19. Is the required Service Line data gathered?
<--- Score

20. Are all team members qualified for all tasks?
<--- Score

21. What qualifications are needed?
<--- Score

22. What is your organizations process which leads to recognition of value generation?
<--- Score

23. Who will gather what data?
<--- Score

24. How are outputs preserved and protected?
<--- Score

25. What is the oversight process?
<--- Score

26. What are your Service Line processes?
<--- Score

27. What are the necessary qualifications?
<--- Score

28. What will drive Service Line change?
<--- Score

29. How is the Service Line Value Stream Mapping managed?
<--- Score

30. What are the revised rough estimates of the financial savings/opportunity for Service Line improvements?
<--- Score

31. How do your work systems and key work processes relate to and capitalize on your core competencies?
<--- Score

32. Were there any improvement opportunities identified from the process analysis?
<--- Score

33. What are your current levels and trends in key measures or indicators of Service Line product and process performance that are important to and

directly serve your customers? How do these results compare with the performance of your competitors and other organizations with similar offerings?
<--- Score

34. What are evaluation criteria for the output?
<--- Score

35. What Service Line metrics are outputs of the process?
<--- Score

36. A compounding model resolution with available relevant data can often provide insight towards a solution methodology; which Service Line models, tools and techniques are necessary?
<--- Score

37. How difficult is it to qualify what Service Line ROI is?
<--- Score

38. How will the data be checked for quality?
<--- Score

39. What Service Line data should be managed?
<--- Score

40. What process improvements will be needed?
<--- Score

41. Is pre-qualification of suppliers carried out?
<--- Score

42. Do your contracts/agreements contain data security obligations?

<--- Score

43. Has an output goal been set?
<--- Score

44. How much data can be collected in the given timeframe?
<--- Score

45. How often will data be collected for measures?
<--- Score

46. How do you use Service Line data and information to support organizational decision making and innovation?
<--- Score

47. What qualifications are necessary?
<--- Score

48. What, related to, Service Line processes does your organization outsource?
<--- Score

49. Who owns what data?
<--- Score

50. Is the gap/opportunity displayed and communicated in financial terms?
<--- Score

51. Do your leaders quickly bounce back from setbacks?
<--- Score

52. Is the performance gap determined?

<--- Score

53. What were the financial benefits resulting from any 'ground fruit or low-hanging fruit' (quick fixes)?
<--- Score

54. How will the Service Line data be captured?
<--- Score

55. What are your current levels and trends in key Service Line measures or indicators of product and process performance that are important to and directly serve your customers?
<--- Score

56. What types of data do your Service Line indicators require?
<--- Score

57. What is the Service Line Driver?
<--- Score

58. What data do you need to collect?
<--- Score

59. Do you understand your management processes today?
<--- Score

60. Do your employees have the opportunity to do what they do best everyday?
<--- Score

61. How was the detailed process map generated, verified, and validated?
<--- Score

62. Do quality systems drive continuous improvement?

<--- Score

63. What methods do you use to gather Service Line data?

<--- Score

64. Can you add value to the current Service Line decision-making process (largely qualitative) by incorporating uncertainty modeling (more quantitative)?

<--- Score

65. What are your best practices for minimizing Service Line project risk, while demonstrating incremental value and quick wins throughout the Service Line project lifecycle?

<--- Score

66. Have any additional benefits been identified that will result from closing all or most of the gaps?

<--- Score

67. Think about some of the processes you undertake within your organization, which do you own?

<--- Score

68. What are your key performance measures or indicators and in-process measures for the control and improvement of your Service Line processes?

<--- Score

69. Who qualifies to gain access to data?

<--- Score

70. An organizationally feasible system request is one that considers the mission, goals and objectives of the organization, key questions are: is the Service Line solution request practical and will it solve a problem or take advantage of an opportunity to achieve company goals?
<--- Score

71. What successful thing are you doing today that may be blinding you to new growth opportunities?
<--- Score

72. How do you define collaboration and team output?
<--- Score

73. What systems/processes must you excel at?
<--- Score

74. Do staff qualifications match your project?
<--- Score

75. How is Service Line data gathered?
<--- Score

76. How do you promote understanding that opportunity for improvement is not criticism of the status quo, or the people who created the status quo?
<--- Score

77. Do you have the authority to produce the output?
<--- Score

78. What are the Service Line design outputs?
<--- Score

79. What are the Service Line business drivers?
<--- Score

80. Where can you get qualified talent today?
<--- Score

81. What is the output?
<--- Score

82. What Service Line data do you gather or use now?
<--- Score

83. Think about the functions involved in your Service Line project, what processes flow from these functions?
<--- Score

84. How do you implement and manage your work processes to ensure that they meet design requirements?
<--- Score

85. What qualifies as competition?
<--- Score

86. What qualifications do Service Line leaders need?
<--- Score

87. What data is gathered?
<--- Score

88. Identify an operational issue in your organization, for example, could a particular task be done more quickly or more efficiently by Service Line?
<--- Score

89. What process should you select for improvement?
<--- Score

90. What are the best opportunities for value improvement?
<--- Score

91. How will corresponding data be collected?
<--- Score

92. What qualifications and skills do you need?
<--- Score

93. What quality tools were used to get through the analyze phase?
<--- Score

94. What are the processes for audit reporting and management?
<--- Score

95. Is the suppliers process defined and controlled?
<--- Score

96. What is the complexity of the output produced?
<--- Score

97. What is the cost of poor quality as supported by the team's analysis?
<--- Score

98. Who gets your output?
<--- Score

99. What training and qualifications will you need?

<--- Score

100. Are your outputs consistent?
<--- Score

101. What were the crucial 'moments of truth' on the process map?
<--- Score

102. Was a cause-and-effect diagram used to explore the different types of causes (or sources of variation)?
<--- Score

103. When should a process be art not science?
<--- Score

104. Is the final output clearly identified?
<--- Score

105. Are all staff in core Service Line subjects Highly Qualified?
<--- Score

106. How will the change process be managed?
<--- Score

107. How many input/output points does it require?
<--- Score

108. How is data used for program management and improvement?
<--- Score

109. Have the problem and goal statements been updated to reflect the additional knowledge gained from the analyze phase?

<--- Score

110. Where is Service Line data gathered?
<--- Score

111. What tools were used to narrow the list of possible causes?
<--- Score

112. Has data output been validated?
<--- Score

113. Were any designed experiments used to generate additional insight into the data analysis?
<--- Score

114. Are Service Line changes recognized early enough to be approved through the regular process?
<--- Score

115. What information qualified as important?
<--- Score

116. Who is involved with workflow mapping?
<--- Score

117. What internal processes need improvement?
<--- Score

118. What conclusions were drawn from the team's data collection and analysis? How did the team reach these conclusions?
<--- Score

119. What does the data say about the performance of the stakeholder process?

<--- Score

120. How is the data gathered?
<--- Score

121. Was a detailed process map created to amplify critical steps of the 'as is' stakeholder process?
<--- Score

122. Have you defined which data is gathered how?
<--- Score

123. How do you measure the operational performance of your key work systems and processes, including productivity, cycle time, and other appropriate measures of process effectiveness, efficiency, and innovation?
<--- Score

124. How is the way you as the leader think and process information affecting your organizational culture?
<--- Score

125. Where is the data coming from to measure compliance?
<--- Score

126. How do you identify specific Service Line investment opportunities and emerging trends?
<--- Score

127. Do you, as a leader, bounce back quickly from setbacks?
<--- Score

128. What did the team gain from developing a sub-process map?
<--- Score

129. What are the disruptive Service Line technologies that enable your organization to radically change your business processes?
<--- Score

130. What controls do you have in place to protect data?
<--- Score

131. Record-keeping requirements flow from the records needed as inputs, outputs, controls and for transformation of a Service Line process, are the records needed as inputs to the Service Line process available?
<--- Score

132. How do you ensure that the Service Line opportunity is realistic?
<--- Score

133. Were Pareto charts (or similar) used to portray the 'heavy hitters' (or key sources of variation)?
<--- Score

134. Is there a strict change management process?
<--- Score

135. Is data and process analysis, root cause analysis and quantifying the gap/opportunity in place?
<--- Score

Add up total points for this section:

_____ = Total points for this section

Divided by: _____ (number of
statements answered) = _____
Average score for this section

Transfer your score to the Service Line
Index at the beginning of the Self-
Assessment.

CRITERION #5: IMPROVE:

INTENT: Develop a practical solution.
Innovate, establish and test the
solution and to measure the results.

In my belief, the answer to this
question is clearly defined:

5 Strongly Agree

4 Agree

3 Neutral

2 Disagree

1 Strongly Disagree

1. How does your organization evaluate strategic
Service Line success?
<--- Score

2. What do you want to improve?
<--- Score

3. Have you identified breakpoints and/or risk
tolerances that will trigger broad consideration of

a potential need for intervention or modification of strategy?

<--- Score

4. How will you know that you have improved?

<--- Score

5. Is the Service Line risk managed?

<--- Score

6. How do you manage Service Line risk?

<--- Score

7. Does a good decision guarantee a good outcome?

<--- Score

8. Is Service Line documentation maintained?

<--- Score

9. Is risk periodically assessed?

<--- Score

10. How scalable is your Service Line solution?

<--- Score

11. What practices helps your organization to develop its capacity to recognize patterns?

<--- Score

12. Risk factors: what are the characteristics of Service Line that make it risky?

<--- Score

13. How will you recognize and celebrate results?

<--- Score

14. What current systems have to be understood and/or changed?
<--- Score

15. Do vendor agreements bring new compliance risk ?
<--- Score

16. Is the Service Line solution sustainable?
<--- Score

17. Risk events: what are the things that could go wrong?
<--- Score

18. What tools were used to evaluate the potential solutions?
<--- Score

19. How do you measure progress and evaluate training effectiveness?
<--- Score

20. What were the criteria for evaluating a Service Line pilot?
<--- Score

21. For decision problems, how do you develop a decision statement?
<--- Score

22. Are events managed to resolution?
<--- Score

23. Which of the recognised risks out of all risks can be most likely transferred?

<--- Score

24. Can you integrate quality management and risk management?
<--- Score

25. Are decisions made in a timely manner?
<--- Score

26. Is the solution technically practical?
<--- Score

27. How do you measure risk?
<--- Score

28. In the past few months, what is the smallest change you have made that has had the biggest positive result? What was it about that small change that produced the large return?
<--- Score

29. What are the expected Service Line results?
<--- Score

30. What risks do you need to manage?
<--- Score

31. What tools do you use once you have decided on a Service Line strategy and more importantly how do you choose?
<--- Score

32. What are the affordable Service Line risks?
<--- Score

33. Is there a high likelihood that any

recommendations will achieve their intended results?
<--- Score

34. Who do you report Service Line results to?
<--- Score

35. Have you achieved Service Line improvements?
<--- Score

36. What improvements have been achieved?
<--- Score

37. How do the Service Line results compare with the performance of your competitors and other organizations with similar offerings?
<--- Score

38. Will the controls trigger any other risks?
<--- Score

39. How will you know when its improved?
<--- Score

40. Are you assessing Service Line and risk?
<--- Score

41. What is the risk?
<--- Score

42. What went well, what should change, what can improve?
<--- Score

43. What assumptions are made about the solution and approach?
<--- Score

44. Risk Identification: What are the possible risk events your organization faces in relation to Service Line?
<--- Score

45. How do you deal with Service Line risk?
<--- Score

46. Was a Service Line charter developed?
<--- Score

47. Who are the Service Line decision-makers?
<--- Score

48. What are the concrete Service Line results?
<--- Score

49. What is the Service Line's sustainability risk?
<--- Score

50. Who controls key decisions that will be made?
<--- Score

51. Are the risks fully understood, reasonable and manageable?
<--- Score

52. What should a proof of concept or pilot accomplish?
<--- Score

53. What can you do to improve?
<--- Score

54. What criteria will you use to assess your Service

Line risks?

<--- Score

55. How are Service Line risks managed?

<--- Score

56. How do you link measurement and risk?

<--- Score

57. Do you have the optimal project management team structure?

<--- Score

58. How does the team improve its work?

<--- Score

59. Are the key business and technology risks being managed?

<--- Score

60. Who are the Service Line decision makers?

<--- Score

61. What strategies for Service Line improvement are successful?

<--- Score

62. How risky is your organization?

<--- Score

63. How do you keep improving Service Line?

<--- Score

64. Where do the Service Line decisions reside?

<--- Score

65. What to do with the results or outcomes of measurements?
<--- Score

66. How do you improve productivity?
<--- Score

67. Who should make the Service Line decisions?
<--- Score

68. If you could go back in time five years, what decision would you make differently? What is your best guess as to what decision you're making today you might regret five years from now?
<--- Score

69. Do you combine technical expertise with business knowledge and Service Line Key topics include lifecycles, development approaches, requirements and how to make a business case?
<--- Score

70. Why improve in the first place?
<--- Score

71. Where do you need Service Line improvement?
<--- Score

72. Can you identify any significant risks or exposures to Service Line third- parties (vendors, service providers, alliance partners etc) that concern you?
<--- Score

73. What tools were most useful during the improve phase?
<--- Score

74. How do you engage, organize your business, develop your service lines?
<--- Score

75. What are the implications of the one critical Service Line decision 10 minutes, 10 months, and 10 years from now?
<--- Score

76. How significant is the improvement in the eyes of the end user?
<--- Score

77. Who controls the risk?
<--- Score

78. Is the measure of success for Service Line understandable to a variety of people?
<--- Score

79. Does the goal represent a desired result that can be measured?
<--- Score

80. Are procedures documented for managing Service Line risks?
<--- Score

81. Which Service Line solution is appropriate?
<--- Score

82. How do you improve your likelihood of success ?
<--- Score

83. How can the phases of Service Line development

be identified?

<--- Score

84. Can the solution be designed and implemented within an acceptable time period?

<--- Score

85. How do you go about comparing Service Line approaches/solutions?

<--- Score

86. What tools were used to tap into the creativity and encourage 'outside the box' thinking?

<--- Score

87. Explorations of the frontiers of Service Line will help you build influence, improve Service Line, optimize decision making, and sustain change, what is your approach?

<--- Score

88. How can you improve performance?

<--- Score

89. Is any Service Line documentation required?

<--- Score

90. What alternative responses are available to manage risk?

<--- Score

91. Are risk management tasks balanced centrally and locally?

<--- Score

92. What are your current levels and trends in key

measures or indicators of workforce and leader development?
<--- Score

93. How can you improve Service Line?
<--- Score

94. How will you know that a change is an improvement?
<--- Score

95. Do those selected for the Service Line team have a good general understanding of what Service Line is all about?
<--- Score

96. Are risk triggers captured?
<--- Score

97. Would you develop a Service Line Communication Strategy?
<--- Score

98. What were the underlying assumptions on the cost-benefit analysis?
<--- Score

99. How will you measure the results?
<--- Score

100. What are the Service Line security risks?
<--- Score

101. Who will be using the results of the measurement activities?
<--- Score

102. How can you better manage risk?
<--- Score

103. What actually has to improve and by how much?
<--- Score

104. Who makes the Service Line decisions in your organization?
<--- Score

105. Is the scope clearly documented?
<--- Score

106. How do you decide how much to remunerate an employee?
<--- Score

107. When you map the key players in your own work and the types/domains of relationships with them, which relationships do you find easy and which challenging, and why?
<--- Score

108. How do you manage and improve your Service Line work systems to deliver customer value and achieve organizational success and sustainability?
<--- Score

109. How is knowledge sharing about risk management improved?
<--- Score

110. Who manages supplier risk management in your organization?
<--- Score

111. How do you improve Service Line service perception, and satisfaction?
<--- Score

112. Is the Service Line documentation thorough?
<--- Score

113. Who manages Service Line risk?
<--- Score

114. For estimation problems, how do you develop an estimation statement?
<--- Score

115. What lessons, if any, from a pilot were incorporated into the design of the full-scale solution?
<--- Score

116. At what point will vulnerability assessments be performed once Service Line is put into production (e.g., ongoing Risk Management after implementation)?
<--- Score

117. Service Line risk decisions: whose call Is It?
<--- Score

118. What is the magnitude of the improvements?
<--- Score

119. Do you cover the five essential competencies: Communication, Collaboration,Innovation, Adaptability, and Leadership that improve an organizations ability to leverage the new Service Line in a volatile global economy?

<--- Score

120. How is continuous improvement applied to risk
management?
<--- Score

121. Who will be responsible for documenting the
Service Line requirements in detail?
<--- Score

122. What Service Line improvements can be made?
<--- Score

123. What needs improvement? Why?
<--- Score

124. To what extent does management recognize
Service Line as a tool to increase the results?
<--- Score

125. Is there any other Service Line solution?
<--- Score

126. What is Service Line risk?
<--- Score

127. Are the most efficient solutions problem-specific?
<--- Score

128. How do you measure improved Service Line
service perception, and satisfaction?
<--- Score

129. Do you need to do a usability evaluation?
<--- Score

130. How are policy decisions made and where?
<--- Score

Add up total points for this section:
_____ = Total points for this section

Divided by: _____ (number of
statements answered) = _____
Average score for this section

Transfer your score to the Service Line
Index at the beginning of the Self-
Assessment.

CRITERION #6: CONTROL:

INTENT: Implement the practical solution. Maintain the performance and correct possible complications.

In my belief, the answer to this question is clearly defined:

5 Strongly Agree

4 Agree

3 Neutral

2 Disagree

1 Strongly Disagree

1. What other systems, operations, processes, and infrastructures (hiring practices, staffing, training, incentives/rewards, metrics/dashboards/scorecards, etc.) need updates, additions, changes, or deletions in order to facilitate knowledge transfer and improvements?
<--- Score

2. You may have created your quality measures at a

time when you lacked resources, technology wasn't up to the required standard, or low service levels were the industry norm. Have those circumstances changed?
<--- Score

3. Does a troubleshooting guide exist or is it needed?
<--- Score

4. How do you establish and deploy modified action plans if circumstances require a shift in plans and rapid execution of new plans?
<--- Score

5. What quality tools were useful in the control phase?
<--- Score

6. How will Service Line decisions be made and monitored?
<--- Score

7. Are you measuring, monitoring and predicting Service Line activities to optimize operations and profitability, and enhancing outcomes?
<--- Score

8. Are the planned controls in place?
<--- Score

9. How will the day-to-day responsibilities for monitoring and continual improvement be transferred from the improvement team to the process owner?
<--- Score

10. How do you plan on providing proper recognition

and disclosure of supporting companies?
<--- Score

11. How will the process owner verify improvement in present and future sigma levels, process capabilities?
<--- Score

12. Will existing staff require re-training, for example, to learn new business processes?
<--- Score

13. Will the team be available to assist members in planning investigations?
<--- Score

14. How likely is the current Service Line plan to come in on schedule or on budget?
<--- Score

15. How do you spread information?
<--- Score

16. How do you encourage people to take control and responsibility?
<--- Score

17. What do you stand for--and what are you against?
<--- Score

18. Do the viable solutions scale to future needs?
<--- Score

19. What is the standard for acceptable Service Line performance?
<--- Score

20. How will the process owner and team be able to hold the gains?
<--- Score

21. Are documented procedures clear and easy to follow for the operators?
<--- Score

22. Who is the Service Line process owner?
<--- Score

23. Is there a documented and implemented monitoring plan?
<--- Score

24. Are operating procedures consistent?
<--- Score

25. Who controls critical resources?
<--- Score

26. What are the critical parameters to watch?
<--- Score

27. Who is going to spread your message?
<--- Score

28. Do you monitor the Service Line decisions made and fine tune them as they evolve?
<--- Score

29. What are the known security controls?
<--- Score

30. What do you measure to verify effectiveness gains?

<--- Score

31. Are controls in place and consistently applied?
<--- Score

32. How do you monitor usage and cost?
<--- Score

33. Are the planned controls working?
<--- Score

34. Who has control over resources?
<--- Score

35. Is reporting being used or needed?
<--- Score

36. Act/Adjust: What Do you Need to Do Differently?
<--- Score

37. Is there a recommended audit plan for routine surveillance inspections of Service Line's gains?
<--- Score

38. Are new process steps, standards, and documentation ingrained into normal operations?
<--- Score

39. Is new knowledge gained imbedded in the response plan?
<--- Score

40. Is there a transfer of ownership and knowledge to process owner and process team tasked with the responsibilities.
<--- Score

41. Is a response plan in place for when the input, process, or output measures indicate an 'out-of-control' condition?
<--- Score

42. Implementation Planning: is a pilot needed to test the changes before a full roll out occurs?
<--- Score

43. How do you plan for the cost of succession?
<--- Score

44. Is there a standardized process?
<--- Score

45. How do you select, collect, align, and integrate Service Line data and information for tracking daily operations and overall organizational performance, including progress relative to strategic objectives and action plans?
<--- Score

46. Has the improved process and its steps been standardized?
<--- Score

47. What is your plan to assess your security risks?
<--- Score

48. How much planning is enough?
<--- Score

49. How do senior leaders actions reflect a commitment to the organizations Service Line values?
<--- Score

50. Will your goals reflect your program budget?
<--- Score

51. How will you measure your QA plan's effectiveness?
<--- Score

52. Against what alternative is success being measured?
<--- Score

53. What should you measure to verify efficiency gains?
<--- Score

54. How can you best use all of your knowledge repositories to enhance learning and sharing?
<--- Score

55. What is your theory of human motivation, and how does your compensation plan fit with that view?
<--- Score

56. Where do ideas that reach policy makers and planners as proposals for Service Line strengthening and reform actually originate?
<--- Score

57. Are pertinent alerts monitored, analyzed and distributed to appropriate personnel?
<--- Score

58. What is the recommended frequency of auditing?
<--- Score

59. Is a response plan established and deployed?
<--- Score

60. What key inputs and outputs are being measured on an ongoing basis?
<--- Score

61. What is the best design framework for Service Line organization now that, in a post industrial-age if the top-down, command and control model is no longer relevant?
<--- Score

62. What are the key elements of your Service Line performance improvement system, including your evaluation, organizational learning, and innovation processes?
<--- Score

63. How do controls support value?
<--- Score

64. Is there an action plan in case of emergencies?
<--- Score

65. How will report readings be checked to effectively monitor performance?
<--- Score

66. Does the response plan contain a definite closed loop continual improvement scheme (e.g., plan-do-check-act)?
<--- Score

67. What can you control?
<--- Score

68. Is there documentation that will support the successful operation of the improvement?
<--- Score

69. How might the group capture best practices and lessons learned so as to leverage improvements?
<--- Score

70. How will input, process, and output variables be checked to detect for sub-optimal conditions?
<--- Score

71. Does the Service Line performance meet the customer's requirements?
<--- Score

72. What are your results for key measures or indicators of the accomplishment of your Service Line strategy and action plans, including building and strengthening core competencies?
<--- Score

73. Will any special training be provided for results interpretation?
<--- Score

74. Is knowledge gained on process shared and institutionalized?
<--- Score

75. Can you adapt and adjust to changing Service Line situations?
<--- Score

76. Does job training on the documented procedures

need to be part of the process team's education and training?
<--- Score

77. What adjustments to the strategies are needed?
<--- Score

78. What are customers monitoring?
<--- Score

79. What is the control/monitoring plan?
<--- Score

80. What Service Line standards are applicable?
<--- Score

81. In the case of a Service Line project, the criteria for the audit derive from implementation objectives, an audit of a Service Line project involves assessing whether the recommendations outlined for implementation have been met, can you track that any Service Line project is implemented as planned, and is it working?
<--- Score

82. What should the next improvement project be that is related to Service Line?
<--- Score

83. Is there a Service Line Communication plan covering who needs to get what information when?
<--- Score

84. What other areas of the group might benefit from the Service Line team's improvements, knowledge, and learning?

<--- Score

85. Can support from partners be adjusted?
<--- Score

86. What are the performance and scale of the Service Line tools?
<--- Score

87. Have new or revised work instructions resulted?
<--- Score

88. Are the Service Line standards challenging?
<--- Score

89. Has the Service Line value of standards been quantified?
<--- Score

90. Are suggested corrective/restorative actions indicated on the response plan for known causes to problems that might surface?
<--- Score

91. What do your reports reflect?
<--- Score

92. How widespread is its use?
<--- Score

93. Is the Service Line test/monitoring cost justified?
<--- Score

94. Do you monitor the effectiveness of your Service Line activities?
<--- Score

95. Who sets the Service Line standards?
<--- Score

96. How will new or emerging customer needs/
requirements be checked/communicated to orient
the process toward meeting the new specifications
and continually reducing variation?
<--- Score

97. Is there a control plan in place for sustaining
improvements (short and long-term)?
<--- Score

98. What are you attempting to measure/monitor?
<--- Score

99. Are there documented procedures?
<--- Score

100. How is Service Line project cost planned,
managed, monitored?
<--- Score

Add up total points for this section:
_ _ _ _ _ = Total points for this section

Divided by: _ _ _ _ _ _ (number of
statements answered) = _ _ _ _ _ _
Average score for this section

Transfer your score to the Service Line
Index at the beginning of the Self-
Assessment.

CRITERION #7: SUSTAIN:

INTENT: Retain the benefits.

In my belief, the answer to this question is clearly defined:

5 Strongly Agree

4 Agree

3 Neutral

2 Disagree

1 Strongly Disagree

1. What trouble can you get into?
<--- Score

2. How many features can be built within a 24-week schedule?
<--- Score

3. Do you think you know, or do you know you know ?
<--- Score

4. Why is it important to have senior management

support for a Service Line project?
<--- Score

5. What happens when a new employee joins the organization?
<--- Score

6. Are you / should you be revolutionary or evolutionary?
<--- Score

7. What types of service lines are missing?
<--- Score

8. Is Service Line realistic, or are you setting yourself up for failure?
<--- Score

9. What are the rules and assumptions your industry operates under? What if the opposite were true?
<--- Score

10. Do you know what you are doing? And who do you call if you don't?
<--- Score

11. What is your Service Line strategy?
<--- Score

12. Do you see more potential in people than they do in themselves?
<--- Score

13. Instead of going to current contacts for new ideas, what if you reconnected with dormant contacts-- the people you used to know? If you were going

reactivate a dormant tie, who would it be?
<--- Score

14. What information is critical to your organization that your executives are ignoring?
<--- Score

15. How do you lead with Service Line in mind?
<--- Score

16. What management system can you use to leverage the Service Line experience, ideas, and concerns of the people closest to the work to be done?
<--- Score

17. Is your strategy driving your strategy? Or is the way in which you allocate resources driving your strategy?
<--- Score

18. If you had to rebuild your organization without any traditional competitive advantages (i.e., no killer technology, promising research, innovative product/ service delivery model, etcetera), how would your people have to approach their work and collaborate together in order to create the necessary conditions for success?
<--- Score

19. Whom among your colleagues do you trust, and for what?
<--- Score

20. How do you maintain Service Line's Integrity?
<--- Score

21. How do you provide a safe environment -physically and emotionally?
<--- Score

22. What are the potential basics of Service Line fraud?
<--- Score

23. Who are your customers?
<--- Score

24. Which Service Line goals are the most important?
<--- Score

25. Can you do all this work?
<--- Score

26. Do you have the right people on the bus?
<--- Score

27. Who is the main stakeholder, with ultimate responsibility for driving Service Line forward?
<--- Score

28. Which functions and people interact with the supplier and or customer?
<--- Score

29. What may be the consequences for the performance of an organization if all stakeholders are not consulted regarding Service Line?
<--- Score

30. Is a Service Line team work effort in place?
<--- Score

31. What are the long-term Service Line goals?
<--- Score

32. How do you go about securing Service Line?
<--- Score

33. How will you insure seamless interoperability of Service Line moving forward?
<--- Score

34. What will be the consequences to the stakeholder (financial, reputation etc) if Service Line does not go ahead or fails to deliver the objectives?
<--- Score

35. What are you challenging?
<--- Score

36. What is your formula for success in Service Line ?
<--- Score

37. Are the assumptions believable and achievable?
<--- Score

38. Who is responsible for Service Line?
<--- Score

39. If there were zero limitations, what would you do differently?
<--- Score

40. How are you doing compared to your industry?
<--- Score

41. In a project to restructure Service Line outcomes, which stakeholders would you involve?

<--- Score

42. What does your signature ensure?
<--- Score

43. What Service Line skills are most important?
<--- Score

44. Who else should you help?
<--- Score

45. Do you think Service Line accomplishes the goals you expect it to accomplish?
<--- Score

46. Why do and why don't your customers like your organization?
<--- Score

47. Who have you, as a company, historically been when you've been at your best?
<--- Score

48. Who will provide the final approval of Service Line deliverables?
<--- Score

49. Why will customers want to buy your organizations products/services?
<--- Score

50. What are internal and external Service Line relations?
<--- Score

51. What new services of functionality will be

implemented next with Service Line ?
<--- Score

52. What are the top 3 things at the forefront of your Service Line agendas for the next 3 years?
<--- Score

53. What is the source of the strategies for Service Line strengthening and reform?
<--- Score

54. Are you maintaining a past–present–future perspective throughout the Service Line discussion?
<--- Score

55. At what moment would you think; Will I get fired?
<--- Score

56. What are specific Service Line rules to follow?
<--- Score

57. How do customers see your organization?
<--- Score

58. What you are going to do to affect the numbers?
<--- Score

59. What is the purpose of Service Line in relation to the mission?
<--- Score

60. What happens at your organization when people fail?
<--- Score

61. Which features are most critical?

<--- Score

62. How do you create buy-in?
<--- Score

63. If no one would ever find out about your accomplishments, how would you lead differently?
<--- Score

64. If you were responsible for initiating and implementing major changes in your organization, what steps might you take to ensure acceptance of those changes?
<--- Score

65. How can you negotiate Service Line successfully with a stubborn boss, an irate client, or a deceitful coworker?
<--- Score

66. How do you keep records, of what?
<--- Score

67. Who will be responsible for deciding whether Service Line goes ahead or not after the initial investigations?
<--- Score

68. Ask yourself: how would you do this work if you only had one staff member to do it?
<--- Score

69. Who, on the executive team or the board, has spoken to a customer recently?
<--- Score

70. Is there a work around that you can use?
<--- Score

71. What are strategies for increasing support and reducing opposition?
<--- Score

72. If your company went out of business tomorrow, would anyone who doesn't get a paycheck here care?
<--- Score

73. Marketing budgets are tighter, consumers are more skeptical, and social media has changed forever the way we talk about Service Line, how do you gain traction?
<--- Score

74. If you had to leave your organization for a year and the only communication you could have with employees/colleagues was a single paragraph, what would you write?
<--- Score

75. What one word do you want to own in the minds of your customers, employees, and partners?
<--- Score

76. What would you recommend your friend do if he/she were facing this dilemma?
<--- Score

77. How do you engage the workforce, in addition to satisfying them?
<--- Score

78. Who is responsible for errors?

<--- Score

79. Which individuals, teams or departments will be involved in Service Line?
<--- Score

80. What is effective Service Line?
<--- Score

81. Do you have past Service Line successes?
<--- Score

82. How do you foster innovation?
<--- Score

83. Is your basic point _____ or _____?
<--- Score

84. How do you govern and fulfill your societal responsibilities?
<--- Score

85. Do you say no to customers for no reason?
<--- Score

86. What was the last experiment you ran?
<--- Score

87. What did you miss in the interview for the worst hire you ever made?
<--- Score

88. Operational - will it work?
<--- Score

89. Who is on the team?

<--- Score

90. What knowledge, skills and characteristics mark a good Service Line project manager?
<--- Score

91. To whom do you add value?
<--- Score

92. Will there be any necessary staff changes (redundancies or new hires)?
<--- Score

93. Where can you break convention?
<--- Score

94. What have you done to protect your business from competitive encroachment?
<--- Score

95. How do you track customer value, profitability or financial return, organizational success, and sustainability?
<--- Score

96. Who do you think the world wants your organization to be?
<--- Score

97. What is the overall business strategy?
<--- Score

98. If you do not follow, then how to lead?
<--- Score

99. Is Service Line dependent on the successful

delivery of a current project?
<--- Score

100. How do you determine the key elements that affect Service Line workforce satisfaction, how are these elements determined for different workforce groups and segments?
<--- Score

101. Who are four people whose careers you have enhanced?
<--- Score

102. Can you maintain your growth without detracting from the factors that have contributed to your success?
<--- Score

103. What is the funding source for this project?
<--- Score

104. Think of your Service Line project, what are the main functions?
<--- Score

105. How do you listen to customers to obtain actionable information?
<--- Score

106. Can the schedule be done in the given time?
<--- Score

107. What is your competitive advantage?
<--- Score

108. What is the range of capabilities?

<--- Score

109. What are you trying to prove to yourself, and how might it be hijacking your life and business success?
<--- Score

110. Is maximizing Service Line protection the same as minimizing Service Line loss?
<--- Score

111. What are the challenges?
<--- Score

112. In retrospect, of the projects that you pulled the plug on, what percent do you wish had been allowed to keep going, and what percent do you wish had ended earlier?
<--- Score

113. Do you have enough freaky customers in your portfolio pushing you to the limit day in and day out?
<--- Score

114. What is the kind of project structure that would be appropriate for your Service Line project, should it be formal and complex, or can it be less formal and relatively simple?
<--- Score

115. What are the business goals Service Line is aiming to achieve?
<--- Score

116. What is your BATNA (best alternative to a negotiated agreement)?
<--- Score

117. What is your question? Why?
<--- Score

118. Are all key stakeholders present at all Structured Walkthroughs?
<--- Score

119. When information truly is ubiquitous, when reach and connectivity are completely global, when computing resources are infinite, and when a whole new set of impossibilities are not only possible, but happening, what will that do to your business?
<--- Score

120. What are the success criteria that will indicate that Service Line objectives have been met and the benefits delivered?
<--- Score

121. How do you manage Service Line Knowledge Management (KM)?
<--- Score

122. How do you transition from the baseline to the target?
<--- Score

123. How can you become the company that would put you out of business?
<--- Score

124. Who will determine interim and final deadlines?
<--- Score

125. How do you accomplish your long range Service

Line goals?
<--- Score

126. Is it economical; do you have the time and money?
<--- Score

127. What is the estimated value of the project?
<--- Score

128. What projects are going on in the organization today, and what resources are those projects using from the resource pools?
<--- Score

129. What trophy do you want on your mantle?
<--- Score

130. How do you foster the skills, knowledge, talents, attributes, and characteristics you want to have?
<--- Score

131. Are you making progress, and are you making progress as Service Line leaders?
<--- Score

132. Whose voice (department, ethnic group, women, older workers, etc) might you have missed hearing from in your company, and how might you amplify this voice to create positive momentum for your business?
<--- Score

133. How do you deal with Service Line changes?
<--- Score

134. If you find that you havent accomplished one of the goals for one of the steps of the Service Line strategy, what will you do to fix it?
<--- Score

135. How much contingency will be available in the budget?
<--- Score

136. How do senior leaders deploy your organizations vision and values through your leadership system, to the workforce, to key suppliers and partners, and to customers and other stakeholders, as appropriate?
<--- Score

137. In the past year, what have you done (or could you have done) to increase the accurate perception of your company/brand as ethical and honest?
<--- Score

138. What goals did you miss?
<--- Score

139. How do you stay inspired?
<--- Score

140. What is an unauthorized commitment?
<--- Score

141. How do you ensure that implementations of Service Line products are done in a way that ensures safety?
<--- Score

142. What are the barriers to increased Service Line production?

<--- Score

143. What relationships among Service Line trends do you perceive?
<--- Score

144. What unique value proposition (UVP) do you offer?
<--- Score

145. If you weren't already in this business, would you enter it today? And if not, what are you going to do about it?
<--- Score

146. Who do you want your customers to become?
<--- Score

147. How do you keep the momentum going?
<--- Score

148. What is the recommended frequency of auditing?
<--- Score

149. What business benefits will Service Line goals deliver if achieved?
<--- Score

150. Political -is anyone trying to undermine this project?
<--- Score

151. What is the craziest thing you can do?
<--- Score

152. How do you set Service Line stretch targets and

how do you get people to not only participate in setting these stretch targets but also that they strive to achieve these?
<--- Score

153. Do you have the right capabilities and capacities?
<--- Score

154. What happens if you do not have enough funding?
<--- Score

155. Are assumptions made in Service Line stated explicitly?
<--- Score

156. What potential megatrends could make your business model obsolete?
<--- Score

157. Who uses your product in ways you never expected?
<--- Score

158. Why is Service Line important for you now?
<--- Score

159. What must you excel at?
<--- Score

160. What would have to be true for the option on the table to be the best possible choice?
<--- Score

161. Who are the key stakeholders?
<--- Score

162. What are the short and long-term Service Line goals?

<--- Score

163. What is a feasible sequencing of reform initiatives over time?

<--- Score

164. What is your area of operation - by service lines?

<--- Score

165. How do you make it meaningful in connecting Service Line with what users do day-to-day?

<--- Score

166. What are current Service Line paradigms?

<--- Score

167. How important is Service Line to the user organizations mission?

<--- Score

168. What Service Line modifications can you make work for you?

<--- Score

169. Which models, tools and techniques are necessary?

<--- Score

170. Are the criteria for selecting recommendations stated?

<--- Score

171. What could happen if you do not do it?
<--- Score

172. Is there any existing Service Line governance structure?
<--- Score

173. How will you motivate the stakeholders with the least vested interest?
<--- Score

174. Why not do Service Line?
<--- Score

175. Where do you as your organization or service line want to be, and will this device help you in that direction?
<--- Score

176. If you got fired and a new hire took your place, what would she do different?
<--- Score

177. Would you rather sell to knowledgeable and informed customers or to uninformed customers?
<--- Score

178. How do you proactively clarify deliverables and Service Line quality expectations?
<--- Score

179. What are your most important goals for the strategic Service Line objectives?
<--- Score

180. How do you know if you are successful?

<--- Score

181. How can you incorporate support to ensure safe and effective use of Service Line into the services that you provide?
<--- Score

182. How can you become more high-tech but still be high touch?
<--- Score

183. How is implementation research currently incorporated into each of your goals?
<--- Score

184. How long will it take to change?
<--- Score

185. Do you feel that more should be done in the Service Line area?
<--- Score

186. What is the overall talent health of your organization as a whole at senior levels, and for each organization reporting to a member of the Senior Leadership Team?
<--- Score

187. What have been your experiences in defining long range Service Line goals?
<--- Score

188. What are your personal philosophies regarding Service Line and how do they influence your work?
<--- Score

189. If your customer were your grandmother, would you tell her to buy what you're selling?
<--- Score

190. What are the key enablers to make this Service Line move?
<--- Score

191. Why should people listen to you?
<--- Score

192. What counts that you are not counting?
<--- Score

Add up total points for this section:
_____ = Total points for this section

Divided by: _____ (number of statements answered) = _____
Average score for this section

Transfer your score to the Service Line Index at the beginning of the Self-Assessment.

Service Line and Managing Projects, Criteria for Project Managers:

1.0 Initiating Process Group: Service Line

1. Have you evaluated the teams performance and asked for feedback?

2. How will you know you did it?

3. How can you make your needs known?

4. Are stakeholders properly informed about the status of the Service Line project?

5. Which of six sigmas dmaic phases focuses on the measurement of internal process that affect factors that are critical to quality?

6. How do you help others satisfy needs?

7. Although the Service Line project manager does not directly manage procurement and contracting activities, who does manage procurement and contracting activities in your organization then if not the PM?

8. How will you do it?

9. During which stage of Risk planning are risks prioritized based on probability and impact?

10. What are the short and long term implications?

11. How is each deliverable reviewed, verified, and validated?

12. What are the required resources?

13. What input will you be required to provide the Service Line project team?

14. Are identified risks being monitored properly, are new risks arising during the Service Line project or are foreseen risks occurring?

15. Who is funding the Service Line project?

16. Establishment of pm office?

17. What will be the pressing issues of tomorrow?

18. Where must it be done?

19. Have requirements been tested, approved, and fulfill the Service Line project scope?

20. How to control and approve each phase?

1.1 Project Charter: Service Line

21. What are the constraints?

22. What are you trying to accomplish?

23. What is the purpose of the Service Line project?

24. Customer benefits: what customer requirements does this Service Line project address?

25. Market – identify products market, including whether it is outside of the objective: what is the purpose of the program or Service Line project?

26. What date will the task finish?

27. What barriers do you predict to your success?

28. Is it an improvement over existing products?

29. What is in it for you?

30. When will this occur?

31. How much?

32. Why executive support?

33. How will you know that a change is an improvement?

34. Strategic fit: what is the strategic initiative identifier for this Service Line project?

35. Who is the Service Line project Manager?

36. Dependent Service Line projects: what Service Line projects must be underway or completed before this Service Line project can be successful?

37. Why Outsource?

38. Why have you chosen the aim you have set forth?

39. What are the known stakeholder requirements?

1.2 Stakeholder Register: Service Line

40. What are the major Service Line project milestones requiring communications or providing communications opportunities?

41. What & Why?

42. How will reports be created?

43. Who is managing stakeholder engagement?

44. Is your organization ready for change?

45. How big is the gap?

46. How should employers make voices heard?

47. How much influence do they have on the Service Line project?

48. Who are the stakeholders?

49. What is the power of the stakeholder?

50. Who wants to talk about Security?

51. What opportunities exist to provide communications?

1.3 Stakeholder Analysis Matrix: Service Line

52. Are there two or three that rise to the top, and a couple that are sliding to the bottom?

53. Location and geographical?

54. Why do you need to manage Service Line project Risk?

55. What are the key services, contractual arrangements, or other relationships between stakeholder groups?

56. What is the stakeholders power and status in relation to the Service Line project?

57. Who are potential allies and opponents?

58. Industry or lifestyle trends?

59. Are the interests in line with the program objectives?

60. Supporters; who are the supporters?

61. What coalitions might build around the issues being tackled?

62. Who influences whom?

63. How to involve media?

64. Marketing - reach, distribution, awareness?

65. Could any of your organizations weaknesses seriously threaten development?

66. Do any safeguard policies apply to the Service Line project?

67. Who has the power to influence the outcomes of the work?

68. Sustainable financial backing?

69. Why involve the stakeholder?

70. Partnership opportunities/synergies?

2.0 Planning Process Group: Service Line

71. Is the schedule for the set products being met?

72. What is the difference between the early schedule and late schedule?

73. How do you integrate Service Line project Planning with the Iterative/Evolutionary SDLC?

74. Is the Service Line project supported by national and/or local organizations?

75. If a risk event occurs, what will you do?

76. If task x starts two days late, what is the effect on the Service Line project end date?

77. How well did the chosen processes fit the needs of the Service Line project?

78. How should needs be met?

79. What types of differentiated effects are resulting from the Service Line project and to what extent?

80. Is the pace of implementing the products of the program ensuring the completeness of the results of the Service Line project?

81. Is the duration of the program sufficient to ensure a cycle that will Service Line project the sustainability

of the interventions?

82. First of all, should any action be taken?

83. You are creating your WBS and find that you keep decomposing tasks into smaller and smaller units. How can you tell when you are done?

84. How will it affect you?

85. Are the necessary foundations in place to ensure the sustainability of the results of the Service Line project?

86. To what extent are the participating departments coordinating with each other?

87. What is involved in Service Line project scope management, and why is good Service Line project scope management so important on information technology Service Line projects?

88. How will users learn how to use the deliverables?

89. In what way has the program contributed towards the issue culture and development included on the public agenda?

2.1 Project Management Plan: Service Line

90. Who is the Service Line project Manager?

91. Are there any windfall benefits that would accrue to the Service Line project sponsor or other parties?

92. How well are you able to manage your risk?

93. What data/reports/tools/etc. do your PMs need?

94. What is risk management?

95. Is the appropriate plan selected based on your organizations objectives and evaluation criteria expressed in Principles and Guidelines policies?

96. Is there an incremental analysis/cost effectiveness analysis of proposed mitigation features based on an approved method and using an accepted model?

97. Is mitigation authorized or recommended?

98. Development trends and opportunities. What if the positive direction and vision of your organization causes expected trends to change?

99. How can you best help your organization to develop consistent practices in Service Line project management planning stages?

100. Are the proposed Service Line project purposes

different than a previously authorized Service Line project?

101. What worked well?

102. Did the planning effort collaborate to develop solutions that integrate expertise, policies, programs, and Service Line projects across entities?

103. Who manages integration?

104. Does the implementation plan have an appropriate division of responsibilities?

105. Are there any client staffing expectations?

106. Are alternatives safe, functional, constructible, economical, reasonable and sustainable?

2.2 Scope Management Plan: Service Line

107. Have stakeholder accountabilities & responsibilities been clearly defined?

108. Is the quality assurance team identified?

109. Has your organization readiness assessment been conducted?

110. Are enough systems & user personnel assigned to the Service Line project?

111. Does the detailed work plan match the complexity of tasks with the capabilities of personnel?

112. Have adequate procedures been put in place for Service Line project communication and status reporting across Service Line project boundaries (for example interdependent software development among interfacing systems)?

113. Have all documents been archived in a Service Line project repository for each release?

114. How many changes are you making?

115. Do you have the reasons why the changes to your organizational systems and capabilities are required?

116. What strengths do you have?

117. Is documentation created for communication with the suppliers and Vendors?

118. Has a proper Service Line project work location been established that will allow the team to work together with user personnel?

119. Have you identified possible roadblocks?

120. When will scope verification be performed?

121. What are the risks that could significantly affect the budget of the Service Line project?

122. Does the Service Line project have a Quality Culture?

123. Are risk triggers captured?

124. What are the risks that could significantly affect the resources needed for the Service Line project?

125. Are you spending the right amount of money for specific tasks?

126. Have all unresolved risks been documented?

2.3 Requirements Management Plan: Service Line

127. Does the Service Line project have a Change Control process?

128. Do you have an agreed upon process for alerting the Service Line project Manager if a request for change in requirements leads to a product scope change?

129. Do you have price sheets and a methodology for determining the total proposal cost?

130. Describe the process for rejecting the Service Line project requirements. Who has the authority to reject Service Line project requirements?

131. Will the contractors involved take full responsibility?

132. Who has the authority to reject Service Line project requirements?

133. How detailed should the Service Line project get?

134. Is it new or replacing an existing business system or process?

135. What are you trying to do?

136. Will you use tracing to help understand the

impact of a change in requirements?

137. Is requirements work dependent on any other specific Service Line project or non-Service Line project activities (e.g. funding, approvals, procurement)?

138. Could inaccurate or incomplete requirements in this Service Line project create a serious risk for the business?

139. To see if a requirement statement is sufficiently well-defined, read it from the developers perspective. Mentally add the phrase, call me when youre done to the end of the requirement and see if that makes you nervous. In other words, would you need additional clarification from the author to understand the requirement well enough to design and implement it?

140. Who is responsible for quantifying the Service Line project requirements?

141. Is stakeholder risk tolerance an important factor for the requirements process in this Service Line project?

142. Why manage requirements?

143. Will you use an assessment of the Service Line project environment as a tool to discover risk to the requirements process?

144. Has the requirements team been instructed in the Change Control process?

145. Will you have access to stakeholders when you

need them?

146. Are actual resources expenditures versus planned expenditures acceptable?

2.4 Requirements Documentation: Service Line

147. Where do system and software requirements come from, what are sources?

148. Where are business rules being captured?

149. Validity. does the system provide the functions which best support the customers needs?

150. Who provides requirements?

151. If applicable; are there issues linked with the fact that this is an offshore Service Line project?

152. Does your organization restrict technical alternatives?

153. Where do you define what is a customer, what are the attributes of customer?

154. What images does it conjure?

155. What are the attributes of a customer?

156. What facilities must be supported by the system?

157. What kind of entity is a problem ?

158. Can the requirements be checked?

159. Is the requirement realistically testable?

160. Has requirements gathering uncovered information that would necessitate changes?

161. Do your constraints stand?

162. What is effective documentation?

163. Who is involved?

164. How do you get the user to tell you what they want?

165. Verifiability. can the requirements be checked?

166. What can tools do for us?

2.5 Requirements Traceability Matrix: Service Line

167. Is there a requirements traceability process in place?

168. Why use a WBS?

169. How small is small enough?

170. What percentage of Service Line projects are producing traceability matrices between requirements and other work products?

171. What are the chronologies, contingencies, consequences, criteria?

172. How will it affect the stakeholders personally in career?

173. Will you use a Requirements Traceability Matrix?

174. Why do you manage scope?

175. What is the WBS?

176. Do you have a clear understanding of all subcontracts in place?

177. Describe the process for approving requirements so they can be added to the traceability matrix and Service Line project work can be performed. Will the Service Line project requirements become approved

in writing?

178. How do you manage scope?

2.6 Project Scope Statement: Service Line

179. What process would you recommend for creating the Service Line project scope statement?

180. Elements that deal with providing the detail?

181. What are the possible consequences should a risk come to occur?

182. What is the most common tool for helping define the detail?

183. Is there a Change Management Board?

184. Are there specific processes you will use to evaluate and approve/reject changes?

185. Will the risk status be reported to management on a regular and frequent basis?

186. Does the scope statement still need some clarity?

187. Is this process communicated to the customer and team members?

188. Will this process be communicated to the customer and Service Line project team?

189. Are there adequate Service Line project control systems?

190. Service Line project lead, team lead, solution architect?

191. Relevant - ask yourself can you get there; why are you doing this Service Line project?

192. Is an issue management process documented and filed?

193. Is the Service Line project organization documented and on file?

194. Will the qa related information be reported regularly as part of the status reporting mechanisms?

195. What are the major deliverables of the Service Line project?

196. Will an issue form be in use?

2.7 Assumption and Constraint Log: Service Line

197. Are there processes in place to ensure internal consistency between the source code components?

198. Does the plan conform to standards?

199. Are there cosmetic errors that hinder readability and comprehension?

200. Are there ways to reduce the time it takes to get something approved?

201. Is the definition of the Service Line project scope clear; what needs to be accomplished?

202. If it is out of compliance, should the process be amended or should the Plan be amended?

203. Have all involved stakeholders and work groups committed to the Service Line project?

204. Can the requirements be traced to the appropriate components of the solution, as well as test scripts?

205. Model-building: what data-analytic strategies are useful when building proportional-hazards models?

206. Does a documented Service Line project organizational policy & plan (i.e. governance model) exist?

207. Is this process still needed?

208. What if failure during recovery?

209. Has a Service Line project Communications Plan been developed?

210. Does the document/deliverable meet all requirements (for example, statement of work) specific to this deliverable?

211. Do the requirements meet the standards of correctness, completeness, consistency, accuracy, and readability?

212. Have Service Line project management standards and procedures been established and documented?

213. Does the traceability documentation describe the tool and/or mechanism to be used to capture traceability throughout the life cycle?

214. Were the system requirements formally reviewed prior to initiating the design phase?

2.8 Work Breakdown Structure: Service Line

215. Can you make it?

216. Is the work breakdown structure (wbs) defined and is the scope of the Service Line project clear with assigned deliverable owners?

217. When does it have to be done?

218. Why is it useful?

219. When do you stop?

220. How far down?

221. What is the probability that the Service Line project duration will exceed xx weeks?

222. Where does it take place?

223. Why would you develop a Work Breakdown Structure?

224. What has to be done?

225. Do you need another level?

226. Who has to do it?

227. When would you develop a Work Breakdown Structure?

228. What is the probability of completing the Service Line project in less that xx days?

229. Is it still viable?

230. How big is a work-package?

2.9 WBS Dictionary: Service Line

231. Actual cost of work performed?

232. Incurrence of actual indirect costs in excess of budgets, by element of expense?

233. Does the scheduling system identify in a timely manner the status of work?

234. Does the contractors system provide for the determination of cost variances attributable to the excess usage of material?

235. Is data disseminated to the contractors management timely, accurate, and usable?

236. Changes in the overhead pool and/or organization structures?

237. Is all budget available as management reserve identified and excluded from the performance measurement baseline?

238. Are meaningful indicators identified for use in measuring the status of cost and schedule performance?

239. Intermediate schedules, as required, which provide a logical sequence from the master schedule to the control account level?

240. Where learning is used in developing underlying budgets is there a direct relationship between

anticipated learning and time phased budgets?

241. Are the responsibilities and authorities of each of the above organizational elements or managers clearly defined?

242. Is the work done on a work package level as described in the WBS dictionary?

243. Are all affected work authorizations, budgeting, and scheduling documents amended to properly reflect the effects of authorized changes?

244. Does the contractors system identify work accomplishment against the schedule plan?

245. Are current budgets resulting from changes to the authorized work and/or internal replanning, reconcilable to original budgets for specified reporting items?

246. Are retroactive changes to BCWS and BCWP prohibited except for correction of errors or for normal accounting adjustments?

247. Are there procedures for monitoring action items and corrective actions to the point of resolution and are corresponding procedures being followed?

248. Is all contract work included in the CWBS?

249. Are the variances between budgeted and actual indirect costs identified and analyzed at the level of assigned responsibility for control (indirect pool, department, etc.)?

250. Does the sum of all work package budgets plus planning packages within control accounts equal the budgets assigned to the already stated control accounts?

2.10 Schedule Management Plan: Service Line

251. Are the schedule estimates reasonable given the Service Line project?

252. Is there a requirements change management processes in place?

253. What is the estimated time to complete the Service Line project if status quo is maintained?

254. Is there an onboarding process in place?

255. Will rolling way planning be used?

256. Has a Service Line project Communications Plan been developed?

257. Is current scope of the Service Line project substantially different than that originally defined?

258. Is quality monitored from the perspective of the customers needs and expectations?

259. Do all stakeholders know how to access this repository and where to find the Service Line project documentation?

260. What happens if a warning is triggered?

261. Were the budget estimates reasonable?

262. Is a pmo (Service Line project management office) in place and provide oversight to the Service Line project?

263. Can be realistically shortened (the duration of subsequent tasks)?

264. Are meeting objectives identified for each meeting?

265. Is the communication plan being followed?

266. Are non-critical path items updated and agreed upon with the teams?

267. Are all key components of a Quality Assurance Plan present?

268. Do Service Line project managers participating in the Service Line project know the Service Line projects true status first hand?

2.11 Activity List: Service Line

269. Are the required resources available or need to be acquired?

270. What did not go as well?

271. For other activities, how much delay can be tolerated?

272. What is the LF and LS for each activity?

273. Who will perform the work?

274. What are you counting on?

275. The wbs is developed as part of a joint planning session. and how do you know that youhave done this right?

276. What went well?

277. How will it be performed?

278. How can the Service Line project be displayed graphically to better visualize the activities?

279. What will be performed?

280. When will the work be performed?

281. What went wrong?

282. What is the probability the Service Line project

can be completed in xx weeks?

283. What went right?

284. Should you include sub-activities?

285. In what sequence?

286. How do you determine the late start (LS) for each activity?

287. Is there anything planned that does not need to be here?

288. How much slack is available in the Service Line project?

2.12 Activity Attributes: Service Line

289. Resource is assigned to?

290. Why?

291. Were there other ways you could have organized the data to achieve similar results?

292. Are the required resources available?

293. Can more resources be added?

294. What conclusions/generalizations can you draw from this?

295. How difficult will it be to complete specific activities on this Service Line project?

296. Has management defined a definite timeframe for the turnaround or Service Line project window?

297. Time for overtime?

298. Where else does it apply?

299. Do you feel very comfortable with your prediction?

300. Does your organization of the data change its meaning?

301. How many days do you need to complete the work scope with a limit of X number of resources?

302. Activity: what is Missing?

303. What is missing?

304. Activity: fair or not fair?

305. Would you consider either of corresponding activities an outlier?

306. Have constraints been applied to the start and finish milestones for the phases?

307. Is there a trend during the year?

2.13 Milestone List: Service Line

308. What background experience, skills, and strengths does the team bring to your organization?

309. Own known vulnerabilities?

310. Who will manage the Service Line project on a day-to-day basis?

311. Which path is the critical path?

312. Usps (unique selling points)?

313. How will the milestone be verified?

314. It is to be a narrative text providing the crucial aspects of your Service Line project proposal answering what, who, how, when and where?

315. Legislative effects?

316. How late can the activity finish?

317. Information and research?

318. How late can each activity be finished and started?

319. Obstacles faced?

320. Describe the concept of the technology, product or service that will be or has been developed. How will it be used?

321. How soon can the activity finish?

322. Timescales, deadlines and pressures?

323. How do you manage time?

324. What specific improvements did you make to the Service Line project proposal since the previous time?

2.14 Network Diagram: Service Line

325. What job or jobs could run concurrently?

326. If the Service Line project network diagram cannot change and you have extra personnel resources, what is the BEST thing to do?

327. What activity must be completed immediately before this activity can start?

328. What is the lowest cost to complete this Service Line project in xx weeks?

329. Planning: who, how long, what to do?

330. Will crashing x weeks return more in benefits than it costs?

331. What can be done concurrently?

332. What must be completed before an activity can be started?

333. What controls the start and finish of a job?

334. Exercise: what is the probability that the Service Line project duration will exceed xx weeks?

335. How confident can you be in your milestone dates and the delivery date?

336. What is the probability of completing the Service Line project in less that xx days?

337. What are the Major Administrative Issues?

338. What are the Key Success Factors?

339. What activities must occur simultaneously with this activity?

340. Review the logical flow of the network diagram. Take a look at which activities you have first and then sequence the activities. Do they make sense?

341. What is the completion time?

342. If x is long, what would be the completion time if you break x into two parallel parts of y weeks and z weeks?

343. What to do and When?

344. Are you on time?

2.15 Activity Resource Requirements: Service Line

345. How do you handle petty cash?

346. Anything else?

347. Why do you do that?

348. What is the Work Plan Standard?

349. Which logical relationship does the PDM use most often?

350. When does monitoring begin?

351. Are there unresolved issues that need to be addressed?

352. Organizational Applicability?

353. Do you use tools like decomposition and rolling-wave planning to produce the activity list and other outputs?

354. Other support in specific areas?

355. What are constraints that you might find during the Human Resource Planning process?

356. How many signatures do you require on a check and does this match what is in your policy and procedures?

2.16 Resource Breakdown Structure: Service Line

357. When do they need the information?

358. How should the information be delivered?

359. Who is allowed to see what data about which resources?

360. Who is allowed to perform which functions?

361. What is your organizations history in doing similar activities?

362. Any changes from stakeholders?

363. Why is this important?

364. What is the purpose of assigning and documenting responsibility?

365. Why time management?

366. What is each stakeholders desired outcome for the Service Line project?

367. What is Service Line project communication management?

368. What are the requirements for resource data?

369. Which resource planning tool provides

information on resource responsibility and accountability?

370. How can this help you with team building?

371. What is the difference between % Complete and % work?

2.17 Activity Duration Estimates: Service Line

372. Does the software appear easy to learn?

373. If Service Line project time and cost are not as important as the number of resources used each month, which is the BEST thing to do?

374. Why is it important to determine activity sequencing on Service Line projects?

375. What is wrong with this scenario?

376. On which process should team members spend the most time?

377. Are costs that may be needed to account for Service Line project risks determined?

378. How can software assist in Service Line project communications?

379. Are Service Line project records organized, maintained, and assessable by Service Line project team members?

380. Service Line project manager is using weighted average duration estimates to perform schedule network analysis. Which type of mathematical analysis is being used?

381. What is the difference between using

brainstorming and the Delphi technique for risk identification?

382. Which type of mathematical analysis is being used?

383. What are the typical challenges Service Line project teams face during each of the five process groups?

384. How does poking fun at technical professionals communications skills impact the industry and educational programs?

385. Are team building activities completed to improve team performance?

386. How difficult will it be to complete specific activities on this Service Line project?

387. Are updates on work results collected and used as inputs to the performance reporting process?

388. Would you rate yourself as being risk-averse, risk-neutral, or risk-seeking?

389. Do procedures exist that identify when and how human resources are introduced and removed from the Service Line project?

390. Are performance reviews conducted regularly to assess the status of Service Line projects?

391. Are procedures defined by which the Service Line project scope may be changed?

2.18 Duration Estimating Worksheet: Service Line

392. What is cost and Service Line project cost management?

393. Why estimate time and cost?

394. Do any colleagues have experience with your organization and/or RFPs?

395. Is the Service Line project responsive to community need?

396. Done before proceeding with this activity or what can be done concurrently?

397. What utility impacts are there?

398. What is your role?

399. Small or large Service Line project?

400. Is a construction detail attached (to aid in explanation)?

401. When does your organization expect to be able to complete it?

402. Science = process: remember the scientific method?

403. What is an Average Service Line project?

404. When, then?

405. Is this operation cost effective?

406. What info is needed?

407. What work will be included in the Service Line project?

408. Value pocket identification & quantification what are value pockets?

2.19 Project Schedule: Service Line

409. How can slack be negative?

410. Why do you think schedule issues often cause the most conflicts on Service Line projects?

411. Are activities connected because logic dictates the order in which others occur?

412. Have all Service Line project delays been adequately accounted for, communicated to all stakeholders and adjustments made in overall Service Line project schedule?

413. What is the difference?

414. Does the condition or event threaten the Service Line projects objectives in any ways?

415. How much detail?

416. Was the Service Line project schedule reviewed by all stakeholders and formally accepted?

417. What does that mean?

418. Change management required?

419. How detailed should a Service Line project get?

420. If you can not fix it, how do you do it differently?

421. How effectively were issues able to be resolved

without impacting the Service Line project Schedule or Budget?

422. Understand the constraints used in preparing the schedule. Are activities connected because logic dictates the order in which others occur?

423. How much slack is available in the Service Line project?

424. Is the structure for tracking the Service Line project schedule well defined and assigned to a specific individual?

425. What is Service Line project management?

426. Are key risk mitigation strategies added to the Service Line project schedule?

2.20 Cost Management Plan: Service Line

427. Service Line project definition & scope?

428. Are vendor contract reports, reviews and visits conducted periodically?

429. Does the Service Line project have a Quality Culture?

430. How relevant is this attribute to this Service Line project or audit?

431. Has the schedule been baselined?

432. Schedule variances – how will schedule variances be identified and corrected?

433. Is it possible to track all classes of Service Line project work (e.g. scheduled, un-scheduled, defect repair, etc.)?

434. Are action items captured and managed?

435. What would the life cycle costs be?

436. Contractors scope – how will contractors scope be defined when contracts are let?

437. Have all necessary approvals been obtained?

438. What will be the split of responsibilities of

progress measurement and controls among the owner, contractor, subcontractors, and vendors?

439. Vac -variance at completion, how much over/ under budget do you expect to be?

440. Are the payment terms being followed?

441. Is the structure for tracking the Service Line project schedule well defined and assigned to a specific individual?

442. Is pert / critical path or equivalent methodology being used?

443. Best practices implementation – How will change management be applied to this Service Line project?

444. Have reserves been created to address risks?

445. Do Service Line project managers participating in the Service Line project know the Service Line projects true status first hand?

2.21 Activity Cost Estimates: Service Line

446. What procedures are put in place regarding bidding and cost comparisons, if any?

447. Certification of actual expenditures?

448. What is the activity recast of the budget?

449. How and when do you enter into Service Line project Procurement Management?

450. Which contract type places the most risk on the seller?

451. What is the activity inventory?

452. Were escalated issues resolved promptly?

453. If you are asked to lower your estimate because the price is too high, what are your options?

454. In which phase of the acquisition process cycle does source qualifications reside?

455. Can you delete activities or make them inactive?

456. Who determines when the contractor is paid?

457. How do you treat administrative costs in the activity inventory?

458. Does the estimator have experience?

459. When do you enter into PPM?

460. Were sponsors and decision makers available when needed outside regularly scheduled meetings?

461. Does the estimator estimate by task or by person?

462. Can you change your activities?

463. What happens if you cannot produce the documentation for the single audit?

2.22 Cost Estimating Worksheet: Service Line

464. How will the results be shared and to whom?

465. Is the Service Line project responsive to community need?

466. What additional Service Line project(s) could be initiated as a result of this Service Line project?

467. Does the Service Line project provide innovative ways for stakeholders to overcome obstacles or deliver better outcomes?

468. What is the purpose of estimating?

469. Will the Service Line project collaborate with the local community and leverage resources?

470. Ask: are others positioned to know, are others credible, and will others cooperate?

471. Can a trend be established from historical performance data on the selected measure and are the criteria for using trend analysis or forecasting methods met?

472. What will others want?

473. What can be included?

474. Identify the timeframe necessary to monitor

progress and collect data to determine how the selected measure has changed?

475. What costs are to be estimated?

476. Is it feasible to establish a control group arrangement?

477. What is the estimated labor cost today based upon this information?

478. What happens to any remaining funds not used?

479. Who is best positioned to know and assist in identifying corresponding factors?

2.23 Cost Baseline: Service Line

480. Have the resources used by the Service Line project been reassigned to other units or Service Line projects?

481. How fast?

482. On budget?

483. Should a more thorough impact analysis be conducted?

484. Has the appropriate access to relevant data and analysis capability been granted?

485. Definition of done can be traced back to the definitions of what are you providing to the customer in terms of deliverables?

486. What is the consequence?

487. Have you identified skills that are missing from your team?

488. For what purpose ?

489. Has the Service Line project (or Service Line project phase) been evaluated against each objective established in the product description and Integrated Service Line project Plan?

490. Impact to environment?

491. Has the Service Line project documentation been archived or otherwise disposed as described in the Service Line project communication plan?

492. Has the Service Line projected annual cost to operate and maintain the product(s) or service(s) been approved and funded?

493. How likely is it to go wrong?

494. Have all approved changes to the Service Line project requirement been identified and impact on the performance, cost, and schedule baselines documented?

495. What deliverables come first?

496. Has training and knowledge transfer of the operations organization been completed?

497. What do you want to measure ?

498. Are there contingencies or conditions related to the acceptance?

2.24 Quality Management Plan: Service Line

499. What are the established criteria that sampling / testing data are compared against?

500. Account for the procedures used to verify the data quality of the data being reviewed?

501. What key performance indicators does your organization use to measure, manage, and improve key processes?

502. How does your organization address regulatory, legal, and ethical compliance?

503. Are there trends or hot spots?

504. Who is approving the QAPP?

505. How is the information recorded?

506. How are senior leaders, employees, and your organization involved in supporting the community?

507. Can you perform this task or activity in a more effective manner?

508. How does your organization decide what to measure?

509. How do you decide what information to record?

510. How do you ensure that your sampling methods and procedures meet your data quality objectives?

511. Who is responsible for approving the qapp?

512. What is the Quality Management Plan?

513. Are you meeting the quality standards?

514. How does your organization establish and maintain customer relationships?

515. Are requirements management tracking tools and procedures in place?

516. How are your organizations compensation and recognition approaches and the performance management system used to reinforce high performance?

517. What is the Difference Between a QMP and QAPP?

518. How long do you retain data?

2.25 Quality Metrics: Service Line

519. Where is quality now?

520. Have risk areas been identified?

521. What forces exist that would cause them to change?

522. Did the team meet the Service Line project success criteria documented in the Quality Metrics Matrix?

523. How should customers provide input?

524. Has risk analysis been adequately reviewed?

525. Are quality metrics defined?

526. How do you know if everyone is trying to improve the right things?

527. Does risk analysis documentation meet standards?

528. Where did complaints, returns and warranty claims come from?

529. What do you measure?

530. What level of statistical confidence do you use?

531. Do the operators focus on determining; is there anything you need to worry about?

532. Have alternatives been defined in the event that failure occurs?

533. How is it being measured?

534. Is a risk containment plan in place?

535. How effective are your security tests?

536. Is there a set of procedures to capture, analyze and act on quality metrics?

537. Was the overall quality better or worse than previous products?

538. Is there alignment within your organization on definitions?

2.26 Process Improvement Plan: Service Line

539. What personnel are the sponsors for that initiative?

540. What actions are needed to address the problems and achieve the goals?

541. Does your process ensure quality?

542. Are you following the quality standards?

543. Have the frequency of collection and the points in the process where measurements will be made been determined?

544. Have storage and access mechanisms and procedures been determined?

545. What is quality and how will you ensure it?

546. To elicit goal statements, do you ask a question such as, What do you want to achieve?

547. Are you making progress on the improvement framework?

548. Management commitment at all levels?

549. Has a process guide to collect the data been developed?

550. The motive is determined by asking, Why do you want to achieve this goal?

551. Why do you want to achieve the goal?

552. Where do you want to be?

553. What is the return on investment?

554. What personnel are the champions for the initiative?

555. Where are you now?

556. What lessons have you learned so far?

557. Are you making progress on the goals?

2.27 Responsibility Assignment Matrix: Service Line

558. Is the anticipated (firm and potential) business base Service Line projected in a rational, consistent manner?

559. What is the primary purpose of the human resource plan?

560. Past experience – the person or the group worked at something similar in the past?

561. Availability – will the group or the person be available within the necessary time interval?

562. What is the business need?

563. Too many rs: with too many people labeled as doing the work, are there too many hands involved?

564. Are your organizations and items of cost assigned to each pool identified?

565. The total budget for the contract (including estimates for authorized and unpriced work)?

566. Direct labor dollars and/or hours?

567. Are management actions taken to reduce indirect costs when there are significant adverse variances?

568. Budgeted cost for work performed?

569. What will the work cost?

570. Does the contractors system provide unit or lot costs when applicable?

571. Why cost benefit analysis?

572. Who is responsible for work and budgets for each wbs?

573. What does wbs accomplish?

574. What expertise is available in your department?

575. Not any rs, as, or cs: if an identified role is only informed, should others be eliminated from the matrix?

576. What do you do when people do not respond?

577. Who is going to do that work?

2.28 Roles and Responsibilities: Service Line

578. What expectations were NOT met?

579. Required skills, knowledge, experience?

580. What expectations were met?

581. What should you highlight for improvement?

582. Who is responsible for each task?

583. Is the data complete?

584. Once the responsibilities are defined for the Service Line project, have the deliverables, roles and responsibilities been clearly communicated to every participant?

585. Does the team have access to and ability to use data analysis tools?

586. What should you do now to prepare for your career 5+ years from now?

587. What areas of supervision are challenging for you?

588. Where are you most strong as a supervisor?

589. Influence: what areas of organizational decision making are you able to influence when you do not

have authority to make the final decision?

590. Are governance roles and responsibilities documented?

591. Who is responsible for implementation activities and where will the functions, roles and responsibilities be defined?

592. How is your work-life balance?

593. Was the expectation clearly communicated?

594. Key conclusions and recommendations: Are conclusions and recommendations relevant and acceptable?

2.29 Human Resource Management Plan: Service Line

595. Are vendor invoices audited for accuracy before payment?

596. Measurable - are the targets measurable?

597. Is there a set of procedures defining the scope, procedures, and deliverables defining quality control?

598. Are Service Line project team members committed fulltime?

599. Cost / benefit analysis?

600. Are the quality tools and methods identified in the Quality Plan appropriate to the Service Line project?

601. What is the boss?

602. Does the business case include how the Service Line project aligns with your organizations strategic goals & objectives?

603. Does the schedule include Service Line project management time and change request analysis time?

604. Are trade-offs between accepting the risk and mitigating the risk identified?

605. Identify who is needed on the core Service

Line project team to complete Service Line project deliverables and achieve its goals and objectives. What skills, knowledge and experiences are required?

606. Pareto diagrams, statistical sampling, flow charting or trend analysis used quality monitoring?

607. Have key stakeholders been identified?

608. Is there any form of automated support for Issues Management?

609. Sensitivity analysis?

610. Is the structure for tracking the Service Line project schedule well defined and assigned to a specific individual?

611. Are post milestone Service Line project reviews (PMPR) conducted with your organization at least once a year?

612. How can below standard performers be guided/ developed to upgrade performance?

613. Has the Service Line project manager been identified?

2.30 Communications Management Plan: Service Line

614. Who have you worked with in past, similar initiatives?

615. Are you constantly rushing from meeting to meeting?

616. What is the stakeholders level of authority?

617. How did the term stakeholder originate?

618. Where do team members get information?

619. Which stakeholders can influence others?

620. Do you feel more overwhelmed by stakeholders?

621. Who needs to know and how much?

622. Are stakeholders internal or external?

623. Are there too many who have an interest in some aspect of your work?

624. Conflict resolution -which method when?

625. How often do you engage with stakeholders?

626. What to know?

627. Are there common objectives between the team

and the stakeholder?

628. How do you manage communications?

629. Who are the members of the governing body?

630. What communications method?

631. Will messages be directly related to the release strategy or phases of the Service Line project?

2.31 Risk Management Plan: Service Line

632. What are the chances the event will occur?

633. Do you have a consistent repeatable process that is actually used?

634. Do benefits and chances of success outweigh potential damage if success is not attained?

635. Have top software and customer managers formally committed to support the Service Line project?

636. What is the impact to the Service Line project if the item is not resolved in a timely fashion?

637. What are it-specific requirements?

638. Market risk -will the new service or product be useful to your organization or marketable to others?

639. Does the software engineering team have the right mix of skills?

640. Why might it be late?

641. Do you train all developers in the process?

642. What will drive change?

643. How is risk response planning performed?

644. Are there risks to human health or the environment that need to be controlled or mitigated?

645. Where do risks appear in the business phases?

646. How much risk can you tolerate?

647. Which is an input to the risk management process?

648. Maximize short-term return on investment?

649. Risk probability and impact: how will the probabilities and impacts of risk items be assessed?

650. How will the Service Line project know if your organizations risk response actions were effective?

651. Methodology: how will risk management be performed on this Service Line project?

2.32 Risk Register: Service Line

652. People risk -are people with appropriate skills available to help complete the Service Line project?

653. What is the appropriate level of risk management for this Service Line project?

654. What may happen or not go according to plan?

655. Is further information required before making a decision?

656. How well are risks controlled?

657. How are risks graded?

658. Financial risk -can your organization afford to undertake the Service Line project?

659. Cost/benefit – how much will the proposed mitigations cost and how does this cost compare with the potential cost of the risk event/situation should it occur?

660. Does the evidence highlight any areas to advance opportunities or foster good relations. If yes what steps will be taken?

661. Risk categories: what are the main categories of risks that should be addressed on this Service Line project?

662. Have other controls and solutions been

implemented in other services which could be applied as an alternative to additional funding?

663. What could prevent you delivering on the strategic program objectives and what is being done to mitigate corresponding issues?

664. What would the impact to the Service Line project objectives be should the risk arise?

665. What evidence do you have to justify the likelihood score of the risk (audit, incident report, claim, complaints, inspection, internal review)?

666. When is it going to be done?

667. What has changed since the last period?

668. Recovery actions - planned actions taken once a risk has occurred to allow you to move on. What should you do after?

669. Amongst the action plans and recommendations that you have to introduce are there some that could stop or delay the overall program?

670. Technology risk -is the Service Line project technically feasible?

2.33 Probability and Impact Assessment: Service Line

671. Is the process supported by tools?

672. Do the requirements require the creation of new algorithms?

673. How do the products attain the specifications?

674. Can the risk be avoided by choosing a different alternative?

675. Are there alternative opinions/solutions/ processes you should explore?

676. Are some people working on multiple Service Line projects?

677. What new technologies are being explored in the same area?

678. Who should be responsible for the monitoring and tracking of the indicators youhave identified?

679. Are enough people available?

680. Do requirements demand the use of new analysis, design, or testing methods?

681. Have you worked with the customer in the past?

682. What is the impact if the risk does occur?

683. Will there be an increase in the political conservatism?

684. Why has this particular mode of contracting been chosen?

685. How much risk do others need to take?

686. How solid is the Service Line projection of competitive reaction?

687. How carefully have the potential competitors been identified?

688. What kind of preparation would be required to do this?

689. Who are the international/overseas Service Line project partners (equipment supplier/supplier/consultant/contractor) for this Service Line project?

2.34 Probability and Impact Matrix: Service Line

690. Are you on schedule?

691. How well is the risk understood?

692. Is a software Service Line project management tool available?

693. How completely has the customer been identified?

694. During which risk management process is a determination to transfer a risk made?

695. Premium on reliability of product?

696. Degree of confidence in estimated size estimate?

697. Do you have a mechanism for managing change?

698. What should be done with risks on the watch list?

699. How is the Service Line project going to be managed?

700. Who is going to be the consortium leader?

701. What things might go wrong?

702. Sensitivity analysis -which risks will have the most impact on the Service Line project?

703. How do you manage Service Line project Risk?

704. Are flexibility and reuse paramount?

705. Why do you need to manage Service Line project Risk?

706. Are you working on the right risks?

707. What is your anticipated volatility of the requirements?

2.35 Risk Data Sheet: Service Line

708. What actions can be taken to eliminate or remove risk?

709. What will be the consequences if the risk happens?

710. Whom do you serve (customers)?

711. What is the chance that it will happen?

712. What is the environment within which you operate (social trends, economic, community values, broad based participation, national directions etc.)?

713. Has a sensitivity analysis been carried out?

714. Are new hazards created?

715. What are the main threats to your existence?

716. What do you know?

717. Who has a vested interest in how you perform as your organization (our stakeholders)?

718. During work activities could hazards exist?

719. Do effective diagnostic tests exist?

720. How can hazards be reduced?

721. What can you do?

722. What will be the consequences if it happens?

723. What can happen?

724. What are you trying to achieve (Objectives)?

725. Will revised controls lead to tolerable risk levels?

726. What if client refuses?

727. What are you here for (Mission)?

2.36 Procurement Management Plan: Service Line

728. Does all Service Line project documentation reside in a common repository for easy access?

729. Have external dependencies been captured in the schedule?

730. Have Service Line project management standards and procedures been identified / established and documented?

731. Have all documents been archived in a Service Line project repository for each release?

732. What were things that you did well, and could improve, and how?

733. Has a capability assessment been conducted?

734. Has the business need been clearly defined?

735. Are procurement deliverables arriving on time and to specification?

736. Is there a procurement management plan in place?

737. Are Service Line project team roles and responsibilities identified and documented?

738. How will the duration of the Service Line project

influence your decisions?

739. Are meeting minutes captured and sent out after meetings?

740. Is the structure for tracking the Service Line project schedule well defined and assigned to a specific individual?

741. Is an industry recognized mechanized support tool(s) being used for Service Line project scheduling & tracking?

2.37 Source Selection Criteria: Service Line

742. What should be considered?

743. What aspects should the contracting officer brief the Service Line project on prior to evaluation of proposals?

744. Who is on the Source Selection Advisory Committee?

745. Are evaluators ready to begin this task?

746. What should be considered when developing evaluation standards?

747. Will the technical evaluation factor unnecessarily force the acquisition into a higher-priced market segment?

748. In the technical/management area, what criteria do you use to determine the final evaluation ratings?

749. How do you facilitate evaluation against published criteria?

750. What is the effect of the debriefing schedule on potential protests?

751. How should the oral presentations be handled?

752. What is cost analysis and when should it be

performed?

753. What procedures are followed when a contractor requires access to classified information or a significant quantity of special material/information?

754. Does your documentation identify why the team concurs or differs with reported performance from past performance report (CPARs, questionnaire responses, etc.)?

755. How will you decide an evaluators write up is sufficient?

756. When is it appropriate to issue a DRFP?

757. How important is cost in the source selection decision relative to past performance and technical considerations?

758. When should debriefings be held and how should they be scheduled?

759. Do you have a plan to document consensus results including disposition of any disagreement by individual evaluators?

760. What risks were identified in the proposals?

761. Is a letter of commitment from each proposed team member and key subcontractor included?

2.38 Stakeholder Management Plan: Service Line

762. Describe the process that will be used to design, develop, review, accept, distribute and change outputs. Will all outputs delivered by the Service Line project follow the same process?

763. Is a stakeholder management plan in place?

764. If a problem has been detected, what tools can be used to determine a root cause?

765. Are mitigation strategies identified?

766. What procedures will be utilised to ensure effective monitoring of Service Line project progress?

767. Are decisions captured in a decisions log?

768. Have the key elements of a coherent Service Line project management strategy been established?

769. Are risk oriented checklists used during risk identification?

770. Have all stakeholders been identified?

771. Is stakeholder involvement adequate?

772. Are Service Line project contact logs kept up to date?

773. What specific resources will be required for implementation activities?

774. Who will be responsible for managing and maintaining the Issues Register?

775. What are the criteria for selecting suppliers of off the shelf products?

776. How is information analyzed, and what specific pieces of data would be of interest to the Service Line project manager?

777. Does the Service Line project have a formal Service Line project Charter?

2.39 Change Management Plan: Service Line

778. How do you gain sponsors buy-in to the communication plan?

779. Have the business unit contacts been selected and notified?

780. How might they respond to the message and if the response may be negative or open to misinterpretation, what else needs to be said?

781. Has a training need analysis been carried out?

782. What policies and procedures need to be changed?

783. Have the systems been configured and tested?

784. Where will the funds come from?

785. When should a given message be communicated?

786. Will the culture embrace or reject this change?

787. Has an information & communications plan been developed?

788. Has the relevant business unit been notified of installation and support requirements?

789. What time commitment will this involve?

790. Will a different work structure focus people on what is important?

791. What risks may occur upfront?

792. Different application of an existing process?

793. Who is the target audience of the piece of information?

794. What are the needs, priorities and special interests of the audience?

795. What will be the preferred method of delivery?

796. How badly can information be misinterpreted?

797. What are the training strategies?

3.0 Executing Process Group: Service Line

798. Does the Service Line project team have enough people to execute the Service Line project plan?

799. How well defined and documented were the Service Line project management processes you chose to use?

800. What factors are contributing to progress or delay in the achievement of products and results?

801. Do Service Line project managers understand your organizational context for Service Line projects?

802. Is activity definition the first process involved in Service Line project time management?

803. What are the main processes included in Service Line project quality management?

804. What areas does the group agree are the biggest success on the Service Line project?

805. When do you share the scorecard with managers?

806. If action is called for, what form should it take?

807. What are the main types of goods and services being outsourced?

808. What communication items need improvement?

809. Does the case present a realistic scenario?

810. What are the main types of contracts if you do decide to outsource?

811. What are some crucial elements of a good Service Line project plan?

812. What are deliverables of your Service Line project?

813. How could stakeholders negatively impact your Service Line project?

814. How can software assist in Service Line project communications?

815. How can software assist in procuring goods and services?

3.1 Team Member Status Report: Service Line

816. Will the staff do training or is that done by a third party?

817. Does every department have to have a Service Line project Manager on staff?

818. How does this product, good, or service meet the needs of the Service Line project and your organization as a whole?

819. The problem with Reward & Recognition Programs is that the truly deserving people all too often get left out. How can you make it practical?

820. How can you make it practical?

821. How it is to be done?

822. Are your organizations Service Line projects more successful over time?

823. Does your organization have the means (staff, money, contract, etc.) to produce or to acquire the product, good, or service?

824. When a teams productivity and success depend on collaboration and the efficient flow of information, what generally fails them?

825. What is to be done?

826. Is there evidence that staff is taking a more professional approach toward management of your organizations Service Line projects?

827. How much risk is involved?

828. What specific interest groups do you have in place?

829. Are the products of your organizations Service Line projects meeting customers objectives?

830. Are the attitudes of staff regarding Service Line project work improving?

831. Why is it to be done?

832. Do you have an Enterprise Service Line project Management Office (EPMO)?

833. How will resource planning be done?

834. Does the product, good, or service already exist within your organization?

3.2 Change Request: Service Line

835. How many lines of code must be changed to implement the change?

836. Are there requirements attributes that are strongly related to the occurrence of defects and failures?

837. Who is communicating the change?

838. Who has responsibility for approving and ranking changes?

839. When to submit a change request?

840. What has an inspector to inspect and to check?

841. Who is responsible to authorize changes?

842. Has the change been highlighted and documented in the CSCI?

843. How do team members communicate with each other?

844. Will this change conflict with other requirements changes (e.g., lead to conflicting operational scenarios)?

845. Why were your requested changes rejected or not made?

846. How are changes graded and who is responsible

for the rating?

847. Describe how modifications, enhancements, defects and/or deficiencies shall be notified (e.g. Problem Reports, Change Requests etc) and managed. Detail warranty and/or maintenance periods?

848. What needs to be communicated?

849. What mechanism is used to appraise others of changes that are made?

850. What are the duties of the change control team?

851. Which requirements attributes affect the risk to reliability the most?

852. Will new change requests be acknowledged in a timely manner?

853. How is the change documented (format, content, storage)?

3.3 Change Log: Service Line

854. Is the requested change request a result of changes in other Service Line project(s)?

855. Is the change request open, closed or pending?

856. How does this relate to the standards developed for specific business processes?

857. Is the submitted change a new change or a modification of a previously approved change?

858. Will the Service Line project fail if the change request is not executed?

859. Does the suggested change request represent a desired enhancement to the products functionality?

860. Where do changes come from?

861. Do the described changes impact on the integrity or security of the system?

862. Who initiated the change request?

863. How does this change affect the timeline of the schedule?

864. Is this a mandatory replacement?

865. Does the suggested change request seem to represent a necessary enhancement to the product?

866. Is the change backward compatible without limitations?

867. Is the change request within Service Line project scope?

868. How does this change affect scope?

869. When was the request submitted?

870. When was the request approved?

3.4 Decision Log: Service Line

871. What alternatives/risks were considered?

872. What is the line where eDiscovery ends and document review begins?

873. Which variables make a critical difference?

874. How does provision of information, both in terms of content and presentation, influence acceptance of alternative strategies?

875. At what point in time does loss become unacceptable?

876. What is your overall strategy for quality control / quality assurance procedures?

877. Is your opponent open to a non-traditional workflow, or will it likely challenge anything you do?

878. How do you know when you are achieving it?

879. Adversarial environment. is your opponent open to a non-traditional workflow, or will it likely challenge anything you do?

880. How effective is maintaining the log at facilitating organizational learning?

881. What is the average size of your matters in an applicable measurement?

882. What are the cost implications?

883. Linked to original objective?

884. What eDiscovery problem or issue did your organization set out to fix or make better?

885. Is everything working as expected?

886. Meeting purpose; why does this team meet?

887. Decision-making process; how will the team make decisions?

888. How do you define success?

889. Does anything need to be adjusted?

890. Who will be given a copy of this document and where will it be kept?

3.5 Quality Audit: Service Line

891. Is there a written procedure for receiving materials?

892. How does the organization know that its industry and community engagement planning and management systems are appropriately effective and constructive in enabling relationships with key stakeholder groups?

893. What data about organizational performance is routinely collected and reported?

894. Are there sufficient personnel having the necessary education, background, training, and experience to assure that all operations are correctly performed?

895. How does your organization know that its system for attending to the health and wellbeing of its staff is appropriately effective and constructive?

896. What review processes are in place for your organizations major activities?

897. How does your organization know that its staff support services planning and management systems are appropriately effective and constructive?

898. Are complaint files maintained?

899. What happens if your organization fails its Quality Audit?

900. Has a written procedure been established to identify devices during all stages of receipt, reconditioning, distribution and installation so that mix-ups are prevented?

901. How does your organization know that its system for staff performance planning and review is appropriately effective and constructive?

902. How does your organization know that its relationships with relevant professional bodies are appropriately effective and constructive?

903. How are you auditing your organizations compliance with regulations?

904. Are adequate and conveniently located toilet facilities available for use by the employees?

905. How does your organization know that it provides a safe and healthy environment?

906. How does your organization know that its relationships with industry and employers are appropriately effective and constructive?

907. How does your organization know that its Strategic Plan is providing the best guidance for the future of your organization?

908. How does your organization know that its staff entrance standards are appropriately effective and constructive and being implemented consistently?

909. Do all staff have the necessary authority and

resources to deliver what is expected of them?

910. How do you indicate the extent to which your personnel would be expected to contribute to the work effort?

3.6 Team Directory: Service Line

911. Is construction on schedule?

912. Decisions: what could be done better to improve the quality of the constructed product?

913. Who are your stakeholders (customers, sponsors, end users, team members)?

914. Who should receive information (all stakeholders)?

915. Days from the time the issue is identified?

916. Process decisions: how well was task order work performed?

917. Process decisions: do invoice amounts match accepted work in place?

918. Who will write the meeting minutes and distribute?

919. What are you going to deliver or accomplish?

920. Process decisions: are contractors adequately prosecuting the work?

921. When will you produce deliverables?

922. Who will report Service Line project status to all stakeholders?

923. How do unidentified risks impact the outcome of the Service Line project?

924. Does a Service Line project team directory list all resources assigned to the Service Line project?

925. Have you decided when to celebrate the Service Line projects completion date?

926. Who are the Team Members?

927. Who will talk to the customer?

928. Decisions: is the most suitable form of contract being used?

929. Timing: when do the effects of communication take place?

3.7 Team Operating Agreement: Service Line

930. What are some potential sources of conflict among team members?

931. How does teaming fit in with overall organizational goals and meet organizational needs?

932. How will you divide work equitably?

933. Do you call or email participants to ensure understanding, follow-through and commitment to the meeting outcomes?

934. Do you post meeting notes and the recording (if used) and notify participants?

935. Must your members collaborate successfully to complete Service Line projects?

936. How will group handle unplanned absences?

937. Did you prepare participants for the next meeting?

938. Do you record meetings for the already stated unable to attend?

939. Communication protocols: how will the team communicate?

940. What are the boundaries (organizational or

geographic) within which you operate?

941. Are there the right people on your team?

942. Do you ask participants to close laptops and place mobile devices on silent on the table while the meeting is in progress?

943. Do you vary your voice pace, tone and pitch to engage participants and gain involvement?

944. What is the number of cases currently teamed?

945. How will you resolve conflict efficiently and respectfully?

946. Resource allocation: how will individual team members account for time and expenses, and how will this be allocated in the team budget?

947. Are there more than two functional areas represented by your team?

948. Do you post any action items, due dates, and responsibilities on the team website?

3.8 Team Performance Assessment: Service Line

949. To what degree can team members frequently and easily communicate with one another?

950. How do you encourage members to learn from each other?

951. Effects of crew composition on crew performance: Does the whole equal the sum of its parts?

952. To what degree are sub-teams possible or necessary?

953. To what degree do team members feel that the purpose of the team is important, if not exciting?

954. To what degree does the teams approach to its work allow for modification and improvement over time?

955. Do you give group members authority to make at least some important decisions?

956. What makes opportunities more or less obvious?

957. To what degree are the goals realistic?

958. To what degree does the teams work approach provide opportunity for members to engage in fact-based problem solving?

959. How do you recognize and praise members for contributions?

960. To what degree will new and supplemental skills be introduced as the need is recognized?

961. Lack of method variance in self-reported affect and perceptions at work: Reality or artifact?

962. To what degree are the skill areas critical to team performance present?

963. To what degree does the teams work approach provide opportunity for members to engage in results-based evaluation?

964. Is there a particular method of data analysis that you would recommend as a means of demonstrating that method variance is not of great concern for a given dataset?

965. Can familiarity breed backup?

966. If you have criticized someones work for method variance in your role as reviewer, what was the circumstance?

967. To what degree can all members engage in open and interactive considerations?

968. Do friends perform better than acquaintances?

3.9 Team Member Performance Assessment: Service Line

969. To what degree does the team possess adequate membership to achieve its ends?

970. To what degree are the goals ambitious?

971. What evidence supports your decision-making?

972. In what areas would you like to concentrate your knowledge and resources?

973. Are the goals SMART ?

974. What were the challenges that resulted for training and assessment?

975. Does adaptive training work?

976. How do you start collaborating?

977. What specific plans do you have for developing effective cross-platform assessments in a blended learning environment?

978. Who should attend?

979. To what degree is the team cognizant of small wins to be celebrated along the way?

980. What changes do you need to make to align practices with beliefs?

981. Are any validation activities performed?

982. What are the staffs preferences for training on technology-based platforms?

983. What are the basic principles and objectives of performance measurement and assessment?

984. What happens if a team member receives a Rating of Unsatisfactory?

985. Is it clear how goals will be accomplished?

986. Are there any safeguards to prevent intentional or unintentional rating errors?

3.10 Issue Log: Service Line

987. Is there an important stakeholder who is actively opposed and will not receive messages?

988. Which stakeholders are thought leaders, influences, or early adopters?

989. Persistence; will users learn a work around or will they be bothered every time?

990. What is the impact on the risks?

991. How is this initiative related to other portfolios, programs, or Service Line projects?

992. What is the status of the issue?

993. Is the issue log kept in a safe place?

994. What are the typical contents?

995. Are the stakeholders getting the information they need, are they consulted, are concerns addressed?

996. Do you prepare stakeholder engagement plans?

997. Why multiple evaluators?

998. Which team member will work with each stakeholder?

999. Who do you turn to if you have questions?

1000. How much time does it take to do it?

4.0 Monitoring and Controlling Process Group: Service Line

1001. Is the program making progress in helping to achieve the set results?

1002. Is progress on outcomes due to your program?

1003. How is agile portfolio management done?

1004. What is the timeline for the Service Line project?

1005. Propriety: who needs to be involved in the evaluation to be ethical?

1006. Feasibility: how much money, time, and effort can you put into this?

1007. Is there sufficient time allotted between the general system design and the detailed system design phases?

1008. Did you implement the program as designed?

1009. Have operating capacities been created and/or reinforced in partners?

1010. How well did you do?

1011. How are you doing?

1012. Overall, how does the program function to serve the clients?

1013. When will the Service Line project be done?

1014. Who needs to be involved in the planning?

1015. Are the services being delivered?

1016. Key stakeholders to work with. How many potential communications channels exist on the Service Line project?

1017. How well defined and documented were the Service Line project management processes you chose to use?

1018. What is the expected monetary value of the Service Line project?

4.1 Project Performance Report: Service Line

1019. To what degree are the teams goals and objectives clear, simple, and measurable?

1020. To what degree are the structures of the formal organization consistent with the behaviors in the informal organization?

1021. To what degree do team members articulate the teams work approach?

1022. To what degree can team members meet frequently enough to accomplish the teams ends?

1023. To what degree does the information network communicate information relevant to the task?

1024. Next Steps?

1025. To what degree does the formal organization make use of individual resources and meet individual needs?

1026. What degree are the relative importance and priority of the goals clear to all team members?

1027. What is the degree to which rules govern information exchange between individuals within your organization?

1028. To what degree do the relationships of the

informal organization motivate taskrelevant behavior and facilitate task completion?

1029. To what degree do team members understand one anothers roles and skills?

1030. To what degree are the tasks requirements reflected in the flow and storage of information?

1031. To what degree can the team ensure that all members are individually and jointly accountable for the teams purpose, goals, approach, and work-products?

1032. To what degree is the information network consistent with the structure of the formal organization?

1033. To what degree will the team ensure that all members equitably share the work essential to the success of the team?

4.2 Variance Analysis: Service Line

1034. Did your organization lose existing customers and/or gain new customers?

1035. Do the rates and prices remain constant throughout the year?

1036. When, during the last four quarters, did a primary business event occur causing a fluctuation?

1037. Why are standard cost systems used?

1038. At what point should variances be isolated and brought to the attention of the management?

1039. Are records maintained to show how undistributed budgets are controlled?

1040. What does an unfavorable overhead volume variance mean?

1041. Does the contractors system include procedures for measuring the performance of critical subcontractors?

1042. How do you evaluate the impact of schedule changes, work around, et?

1043. Contemplated overhead expenditure for each period based on the best information currently is available?

1044. How does your organization measure

performance?

1045. Are data elements reconcilable between internal summary reports and reports forwarded to the stakeholders?

1046. Is the entire contract planned in time-phased control accounts to the extent practicable?

1047. Who are responsible for the establishment of budgets and assignment of resources for overhead performance?

1048. Are indirect costs charged to the appropriate indirect pools and incurring organization?

1049. Are there knowledgeable Service Line projections of future performance?

1050. Are all cwbs elements specified for external reporting?

1051. Are there changes in the direct base to which overhead costs are allocated?

1052. Are overhead cost budgets established for each department which has authority to incur overhead costs?

4.3 Earned Value Status: Service Line

1053. Are you hitting your Service Line projects targets?

1054. Verification is a process of ensuring that the developed system satisfies the stakeholders agreements and specifications; Are you building the product right? What do you verify?

1055. Validation is a process of ensuring that the developed system will actually achieve the stakeholders desired outcomes; Are you building the right product? What do you validate?

1056. What is the unit of forecast value?

1057. Where is evidence-based earned value in your organization reported?

1058. How does this compare with other Service Line projects?

1059. How much is it going to cost by the finish?

1060. Where are your problem areas?

1061. Earned value can be used in almost any Service Line project situation and in almost any Service Line project environment. it may be used on large Service Line projects, medium sized Service Line projects, tiny Service Line projects (in cut-down form), complex and simple Service Line projects and in any market sector. some people, of course, know all about earned value, they have used it for years - but perhaps not as effectively as they could have?

1062. When is it going to finish?

1063. If earned value management (EVM) is so good in determining the true status of a Service Line project and Service Line project its completion, why is it that hardly any one uses it in information systems related Service Line projects?

4.4 Risk Audit: Service Line

1064. Are all financial transactions accurately recorded (receipted, banked)?

1065. To what extent should analytical procedures be utilized in the risk-assessment process?

1066. Have all possible risks/hazards been identified (including injury to staff, damage to equipment, impact on others in the community)?

1067. What effect would a better risk management program have had?

1068. Are all managers or operators of the facility or equipment competent or qualified?

1069. Is the auditor truly independent?

1070. From an empirical perspective, does the business risk approach lead to a more effective audit, or simply to increased consulting revenue detrimental to audit rigor?

1071. Is your organization willing to commit significant time to the requirements gathering process?

1072. How do you prioritize risks?

1073. Do requirements put excessive performance constraints on the product?

1074. If applicable; does the software interface with new or unproven hardware or unproven vendor products?

1075. What can you do to manage outcomes?

1076. When your organization is entering into a major contract, does it seek legal advice?

1077. What is happening in other jurisdictions? Could that happen here?

1078. Do you have an emergency plan?

1079. How can the strategy fail/achieved?

1080. Are you willing to seek legal advice when required?

1081. Will participants be required to sign a legally counselled waiver or risk disclaimer when entering an event?

1082. Improving fraud detection: do auditors react to abnormal inconsistencies between financial and non-financial measures?

1083. What impact does experience with one client have on decisions made for other clients during the risk-assessment process?

4.5 Contractor Status Report: Service Line

1084. Are there contractual transfer concerns?

1085. What was the actual budget or estimated cost for your organizations services?

1086. What process manages the contracts?

1087. Describe how often regular updates are made to the proposed solution. Are corresponding regular updates included in the standard maintenance plan?

1088. How is risk transferred?

1089. What was the final actual cost?

1090. How long have you been using the services?

1091. How does the proposed individual meet each requirement?

1092. What is the average response time for answering a support call?

1093. What are the minimum and optimal bandwidth requirements for the proposed solution?

1094. Who can list a Service Line project as organization experience, your organization or a previous employee of your organization?

1095. What was the budget or estimated cost for your organizations services?

1096. If applicable; describe your standard schedule for new software version releases. Are new software version releases included in the standard maintenance plan?

1097. What was the overall budget or estimated cost?

4.6 Formal Acceptance: Service Line

1098. Did the Service Line project manager and team act in a professional and ethical manner?

1099. Did the Service Line project achieve its MOV?

1100. Does it do what Service Line project team said it would?

1101. How does your team plan to obtain formal acceptance on your Service Line project?

1102. Have all comments been addressed?

1103. What was done right?

1104. How well did the team follow the methodology?

1105. What lessons were learned about your Service Line project management methodology?

1106. Was the sponsor/customer satisfied?

1107. What function(s) does it fill or meet?

1108. Do you buy pre-configured systems or build your own configuration?

1109. What can you do better next time?

1110. Who supplies data?

1111. Is formal acceptance of the Service Line project

product documented and distributed?

1112. Was the client satisfied with the Service Line project results?

1113. Was the Service Line project work done on time, within budget, and according to specification?

1114. Does it do what client said it would?

1115. Who would use it?

1116. Do you buy-in installation services?

1117. Was the Service Line project goal achieved?

5.0 Closing Process Group: Service Line

1118. Was the user/client satisfied with the end product?

1119. What is the Service Line project name and date of completion?

1120. How well defined and documented were the Service Line project management processes you chose to use?

1121. Will the Service Line project deliverable(s) replace a current asset or group of assets?

1122. What can you do better next time, and what specific actions can you take to improve?

1123. Is the Service Line project funded?

1124. How well did the chosen processes produce the expected results?

1125. What is the Service Line project Management Process?

1126. Specific - is the objective clear in terms of what, how, when, and where the situation will be changed?

1127. Did you do what you said you were going to do?

1128. How will staff learn how to use the deliverables?

1129. What do you need to do?

1130. Did the Service Line project team have the right skills?

1131. Was the schedule met?

1132. What were things that you did very well and want to do the same again on the next Service Line project?

1133. What was learned?

1134. Does the close educate others to improve performance?

1135. Did you do things well?

1136. What could be done to improve the process?

5.1 Procurement Audit: Service Line

1137. Does the manual contain policies relating to all business management functions?

1138. Is the routing of copies of purchase order forms defined?

1139. Is the purchasing department responsible for a continual review of marketing trends, particularly on long-term contracts and contracts containing escalation clauses?

1140. Are all purchase orders accounted for?

1141. Have late payment interests been rewarded and could they have been avoided?

1142. Is there no evidence of any external or superior pressure to reach a specific result?

1143. What is the process cost of the procurement function?

1144. Does the individual having check-signing responsibility review the use of the signature plates?

1145. Where funding is being arranged by borrowings, do corresponding have the necessary approval and legal authority?

1146. Is there any objection?

1147. Are there appropriate controls in place to

ensure that the procurement Service Line project complies with relevant legislation?

1148. Is there time waste during tendering?

1149. Are petty cash funds operated on an imprest basis?

1150. Does the contract include performance-based clauses?

1151. Are goods generally ordered and received in time to be used in the programs for which they were ordered?

1152. Does your organization have an overall strategy and/or policy on public procurement, providing guidance for procuring entities?

1153. Are open purchase orders with a fixed monetary limitation used for local purchases of small dollar value?

1154. Do appropriate controls ensure that procurement decisions are not biased by conflicts of interest or corruption?

1155. Has your organization clearly defined the award criteria?

1156. Are all purchase orders signed by the purchasing agent?

5.2 Contract Close-Out: Service Line

1157. Are the signers the authorized officials?

1158. Have all contract records been included in the Service Line project archives?

1159. Parties: Authorized?

1160. Was the contract complete without requiring numerous changes and revisions?

1161. How is the contracting office notified of the automatic contract close-out?

1162. Parties: who is involved?

1163. Change in attitude or behavior?

1164. Have all acceptance criteria been met prior to final payment to contractors?

1165. How/when used ?

1166. Was the contract type appropriate?

1167. What happens to the recipient of services?

1168. Has each contract been audited to verify acceptance and delivery?

1169. Have all contracts been closed?

1170. Was the contract sufficiently clear so as not to

result in numerous disputes and misunderstandings?

1171. How does it work?

1172. Change in circumstances?

1173. What is capture management?

1174. Have all contracts been completed?

1175. Change in knowledge?

5.3 Project or Phase Close-Out: Service Line

1176. What was expected from each stakeholder?

1177. Have business partners been involved extensively, and what data was required for them?

1178. What security considerations needed to be addressed during the procurement life cycle?

1179. What is the information level of detail required for each stakeholder?

1180. What is a Risk Management Process?

1181. Were the outcomes different from the already stated planned?

1182. What advantages do the an individual interview have over a group meeting, and vice-versa?

1183. How much influence did the stakeholder have over others?

1184. In preparing the Lessons Learned report, should it reflect a consensus viewpoint, or should the report reflect the different individual viewpoints?

1185. What are the informational communication needs for each stakeholder?

1186. Planned completion date?

1187. Who controlled the resources for the Service Line project?

1188. What could have been improved?

1189. What information did each stakeholder need to contribute to the Service Line projects success?

1190. Who exerted influence that has positively affected or negatively impacted the Service Line project?

1191. Did the delivered product meet the specified requirements and goals of the Service Line project?

1192. Planned remaining costs?

5.4 Lessons Learned: Service Line

1193. How well do you feel the executives supported this Service Line project?

1194. How effective were your design reviews?

1195. How efficient were Service Line project team meetings conducted?

1196. Would you spend your own time fixing this issue?

1197. Is there a clear cause and effect between the activity and the lesson learned?

1198. How mature are the observations?

1199. What were the main bottlenecks on the process?

1200. How effective were the communications materials in providing and orienting team members about the details of the Service Line project?

1201. How effective was the training you received in preparation for the use of the product/service?

1202. What is the impact of tax policy on the case?

1203. Would you spend your own money to fix this issue?

1204. What are the needs of the individuals?

1205. How useful was your testing?

1206. How efficient and effective were Service Line project team meetings?

1207. How useful was the content of the training you received in preparation for the use of the product/ service?

1208. How well were expectations met regarding the frequency and content of information that was conveyed to by the Service Line project Manager?

1209. Were quality procedures built into the Service Line project?

1210. What was the methodology behind successful learning experiences, and how might they be applied to the broader challenge of your organizations knowledge management?

1211. How well does the product or service the Service Line project produced meet the defined Service Line project requirements?

1212. Where do you go from here?

Index

CPSIA information can be obtained
at www.ICGtesting.com
Printed in the USA
BVHW041215170719
553686BV00012B/347/P